Instagram Income:

A Guide to Building Passive Wealth with Evergreen Content, Digital Courses, and Automated Affiliate Marketing on Social Media

Chris Kirton

Table of Contents

Introduction:

What if the platform you scroll through daily could become your goldmine? Imagine transforming Instagram from a time-consuming hobby into a powerful engine of passive wealth. Not just a side hustle, but a sustainable business that runs while you sleep, delivering financial freedom and the flexibility to live life on your terms.

This isn't a pipe dream or a promise of overnight success. It's the result of a strategic approach to leveraging Instagram's untapped potential. Welcome to Instagram Income: A Guide to Building Passive Wealth with Evergreen Content, Digital Courses, and Automated Affiliate Marketing on Social Media.

This book isn't about amassing a million followers or going viral. It's about creating a system—a well-oiled machine that works for you. Whether you're a content creator, a small business owner, or just someone eager to escape the grind of a 9-to-5 job, this guide will show you how to turn Instagram into your most profitable asset.

The New Era of Social Media Wealth

Social media isn't just a tool for connection; it's a marketplace, an education hub, and a source of inspiration. Instagram, with its billion-plus users, stands at the forefront of this digital revolution. Yet, most users remain spectators, scrolling past opportunities without ever realizing their potential.

The magic lies in Instagram's unique ability to combine visual storytelling with direct engagement. Unlike other platforms, Instagram allows you to cultivate a loyal community that feels personally connected to you. When done right, this connection translates into trust—and trust is the cornerstone of any successful business.

But here's the secret sauce: while most people hustle for likes and comments, the true wealth builders focus on systems. They create content that stays relevant (evergreen), develop digital products that solve problems, and partner with brands through affiliate marketing—all while setting up automation that minimizes effort and maximizes returns.

Why Passive Income? Why Now?

The world is changing. Job security isn't what it used to be, and the traditional notion of trading hours for dollars is fading fast. Passive income is no longer a luxury—it's a necessity for financial freedom.

Instagram offers a unique advantage: it's accessible to anyone, regardless of location, industry, or experience level. With the right strategies, you can monetize your expertise, passions, or even your hobbies. From fitness coaches to fashion enthusiasts, from educators to tech geeks—there's room for everyone.

This book will guide you through the three pillars of Instagram income:

- **Evergreen Content**: Posts, reels, and stories that generate engagement long after you've hit "publish."
- **Digital Courses**: Scalable products that allow you to share your knowledge with thousands of eager learners.
- **Automated Affiliate Marketing**: Partnering with brands and earning commissions through systems that require minimal effort.

What You'll Learn

This isn't a theoretical guide filled with abstract ideas. It's a practical, step-by-step playbook designed to help you succeed. You'll learn how to:

- Define your niche and build an authentic personal brand.
- Create content that captivates and converts.
- Design, market, and sell digital courses that provide lasting value.
- Partner with brands that align with your audience's needs.
- Set up systems that run 24/7, allowing you to focus on what matters most.

A Journey Worth Taking

The path to passive income on Instagram isn't always smooth, but it's worth every step. As you turn these pages, you'll discover stories of real people who started with nothing more than an idea and a smartphone—and went on to build thriving businesses.

Are you ready to unlock the full potential of Instagram? Are you ready to stop scrolling and start building?

Let's dive in. Your journey to financial freedom begins here.

Chapter 1: Laying the Foundation

Before you build a business on Instagram, you need a solid foundation—one that's more than just a pretty feed or a catchy bio. True success on this platform starts with clarity: knowing who you are, what you stand for, and who you're speaking to. Without these elements, your efforts risk getting lost in the noise of 1.3 billion active users.

This chapter is about creating that foundation. It's not glamorous, but it's essential. Think of it like laying the groundwork for a skyscraper. The taller the building, the deeper the foundation must go.

Finding Your Niche: What Do You Stand For?

If Instagram is a marketplace, your niche is your storefront. It's the specific corner of the market where you shine. But finding your niche is more than picking a trendy topic or mimicking others. It's about uncovering the intersection of three things:

- **Your Passion**: What lights you up? Fitness? Travel? Parenting? Think about topics you could talk about endlessly without running out of energy.
- **Your Expertise**: What do you know well enough to teach or share? This could be skills from your day job, a hobby you've mastered, or personal experiences that give you unique insight.

- **Market Demand**: What are people actively searching for on Instagram? Use hashtags, explore questions in comments, or use Instagram's search bar to uncover trending interests.

Your niche should feel authentic to you and align with what your audience wants. For example, a fitness coach might narrow their niche from "general fitness" to "postpartum workouts for new moms." The smaller the niche, the more specific your audience—and the easier it is to stand out.

Building a Brand That Resonates

A brand is more than a logo or a color scheme; it's the emotional connection people feel when they interact with you. On Instagram, your brand is your identity. It's the consistent tone, style, and message you convey across every post, story, and DM.

Start by answering these questions:

- What do I want people to feel when they see my content? (Inspired? Empowered? Entertained?)
- What values drive my message? (Authenticity? Growth? Fun?)
- What's my unique voice? (Warm and approachable? Professional and insightful?)

Your brand should be a reflection of you. Don't try to appeal to everyone—speak directly to your ideal audience.

Setting Up Your Profile for Success

Your Instagram profile is your first impression. In seconds, visitors decide whether to follow you or move on. Make every element count:

- **Profile Photo**: Choose a clear, high-quality image that reflects your personality. If you're a brand, use a logo; if you're a creator, use a smiling photo.
- **Bio**: Your bio should tell visitors who you are, what you offer, and why they should follow you. For example: "Helping busy moms lose weight with 20-min home workouts. DM for free resources!"
- **Call to Action**: Include a clickable link with a clear call-to-action (CTA). This could lead to a free resource, a course, or an affiliate product. Use tools like Linktree to consolidate multiple links.

The Power of Consistency

The final piece of your foundation is consistency. Consistency builds trust, and trust builds followers. Decide on a posting schedule you can stick to—whether it's daily, three times a week, or weekly. Consistency isn't just about timing; it's about delivering quality content that aligns with your brand.

With a strong foundation in place, you're ready to build your Instagram empire. The skyscraper of your dreams is within reach—one post at a time.

1.1 Defining Your Niche: What Do You Stand For

Imagine stepping into a bustling marketplace. Stalls line the street, each vying for attention. Some vendors shout their offers to anyone within earshot, while others quietly wait for customers to wander by. Then there's one vendor whose stall is unlike the rest. Their display is curated with precision, their message is clear, and they seem to know exactly who their customers are. That's the power of defining your niche on Instagram.

A niche isn't just a topic or category; it's a promise. It's your declaration to the world about who you are, what you stand for, and the unique value you bring. In an environment as crowded as Instagram, your niche is your lighthouse, cutting through the fog of generic content and guiding the right people—your people—toward you.

The Sweet Spot: Passion, Expertise, and Demand

Your niche lives at the intersection of three key elements:

- **Your Passion**: Start with what excites you. Your passion is the fuel that will keep you going when the novelty of posting wears off. Ask yourself, What do I love talking about? What could I create content about for years without losing interest? Whether it's cooking, personal finance, or sustainable living, your passion ensures authenticity and enthusiasm.
- **Your Expertise**: Passion alone isn't enough. To stand out, you need to provide value—and that comes from expertise. Expertise doesn't mean being the world's leading authority; it means knowing more than the average person and being willing to share that knowledge. What have you studied, practiced, or experienced that gives you insight others lack?
- **Market Demand**: Finally, your niche must align with what people want or need. It doesn't matter how passionate or knowledgeable you are if no one is looking for content in your chosen area. Research hashtags, explore trending topics, and analyze your potential audience's questions or pain points. What problems can you solve for them?

The Perils of Being Too Broad

Many new creators make the mistake of keeping their niche too broad, fearing that specificity will limit their audience. But the truth is, when you try to appeal to everyone, you appeal to no one. A vague niche—like "fitness" or "travel"—lacks the magnetism needed to draw in a loyal following.

Instead, narrow your focus. Are you a fitness coach specializing in workouts for people over 50? A traveler who shares tips for solo women exploring off-the-beaten-path destinations? The more specific your niche, the more likely you'll attract an audience that feels like your content was made just for them.

Refining Your Message

Once you've identified your niche, craft a clear, concise message that encapsulates it. Think of it as your elevator pitch—the 10-second statement that explains who you are and what you offer. For example:

- "Helping busy professionals stay fit with 30-minute home workouts."
- "Simplifying eco-friendly living for families."
- "Inspiring budget-conscious travelers to explore the world."

Your message should resonate with your audience and reflect your unique perspective.

Staying True to Your Niche

Your niche is your North Star, but that doesn't mean you can't evolve. As your audience grows, you might refine your focus or expand into related areas. Just remember: consistency builds trust. Stay true to what you stand for, and your audience will stay true to you.

With your niche defined, you're no longer shouting into the void. You've found your voice, your people, and your purpose. Now it's time to turn that clarity into content that captivates and converts.

1.2 Building a Brand That Resonates

On Instagram, a brand is more than a logo, color scheme, or tagline. It's a feeling. It's the emotional connection that your audience experiences when they interact with your content. A resonant brand doesn't just attract followers—it builds a community of loyal advocates who believe in what you stand for and trust in what you offer.

But how do you create a brand that truly resonates? It begins with understanding that your brand is a reflection of you, your values, and the people you aim to serve.

Step 1: Define Your Core Values

Your brand's foundation lies in its values. What do you stand for? What principles guide your decisions and actions? For example, if you're a wellness coach, your core values might include empowerment, balance, and sustainability. These values should permeate every aspect of your brand—from your captions to your collaborations.

Take a moment to write down three to five core values that define your approach. These aren't just words; they're the essence of your brand's identity. When your audience recognizes and connects with these values, they're more likely to trust you and stick around.

Step 2: Craft Your Brand Voice

Your brand voice is how you "speak" to your audience. It's the personality of your words, and it needs to align with your values and your audience. Are you professional and insightful, like a trusted advisor? Warm and approachable, like a close friend? Or perhaps bold and edgy, pushing boundaries and challenging norms?

Once you've identified your voice, be consistent. Consistency doesn't mean being rigid; it means maintaining a recognizable tone that feels authentic. For example, if you're playful and casual in your posts, your direct messages and email copy should match that energy.

Step 3: Visual Identity: More Than Pretty Pictures

Instagram is a visual platform, and your aesthetic is often the first thing people notice. But don't mistake aesthetics for vanity—it's about creating a cohesive experience that reinforces your message.

Start with your color palette. Choose 3-5 colors that reflect your brand's vibe. A financial coach might use calming blues and grays to convey trust and professionalism, while a lifestyle influencer might opt for vibrant pinks and yellows to radiate energy and positivity.

Your visuals should also include consistent fonts, filters, and imagery. However, don't get so caught up in perfection that you lose your authenticity. A beautifully curated feed is meaningless if it doesn't feel real.

Step 4: Tell a Story

People connect with stories, not sales pitches. Your brand isn't just about what you do—it's about why you do it. Share your journey, struggles, and triumphs. Why did you start this Instagram page? What do you hope to achieve?

For example, if you're a fitness trainer, talk about your transformation or a time you overcame challenges in your health journey. Let your audience see the human behind the posts.

Step 5: Know Your Audience

A brand that resonates speaks directly to its audience's needs, dreams, and pain points. Spend time understanding who your followers are and what they care about. Use Instagram's tools—polls, questions, and comments—to ask them directly.

When you create content that feels like it's tailored just for them, you create trust. And trust is the currency of Instagram's success.

Step 6: Evolve Without Losing Yourself

A resonant brand grows with its audience. Trends shift, algorithms change, and so do people's interests. The key is to evolve without straying from your core values. If you stay true to what makes your brand unique, your audience will follow you through every evolution.

A brand that resonates isn't built overnight, but when done right, it becomes your greatest asset. It transforms followers into fans, skeptics into believers, and casual viewers into loyal customers. And it all starts with understanding who you are and staying true to it.

1.3 Setting Up Your Instagram Profile for Success

Your Instagram profile is your digital storefront, the first impression that tells visitors whether they should stick around or move on. It's not just a placeholder for your username and a cute bio—it's your elevator pitch, your handshake, and your business card all rolled into one. A well-optimized profile can be the difference between a fleeting glance and a loyal follower.

This chapter breaks down the elements of an Instagram profile that captivates, converts, and communicates your brand's value in seconds.

1. Choose the Right Profile Picture

Your profile picture is often the first thing people notice, so it needs to be clear, professional, and reflective of your brand.

- **Personal Brand**: If you're building a personal brand, a high-quality photo of yourself works best. Choose an image with good lighting, a warm smile, and minimal distractions. This helps establish trust and relatability.
- **Business or Product Brand**: Use a logo that's simple, recognizable, and aligns with your brand colors. Avoid overly complex designs that may be hard to see in the small profile circle.

Remember, your profile picture appears everywhere—from comments to DMs—so make it memorable.

2. Create a Captivating Bio

Your bio is your chance to make a strong first impression. You have just 150 characters to communicate who you are, what you offer, and why people should follow you.

Here's a formula that works:

[Who you are] + [What you do] + [How you help your audience] + [Call-to-action (CTA)]

For example:

- "Helping busy moms lose weight with 20-min home workouts | Free meal plan below ↓"
- "Teaching entrepreneurs to grow their biz with Instagram | DM 'start' for tips!"

Use emojis sparingly to add personality and clarity, but don't overdo it—keep it clean and professional.

3. Optimize Your Username and Handle

Your username (@handle) and name field are searchable, so use them strategically.

- **Username**: Keep it simple, memorable, and aligned with your brand. Avoid random numbers or special characters that make it harder to find you.

- **Name Field**: This is prime real estate for keywords. For example, if you're a digital marketer, your name field could read: "Sarah | Instagram Marketing." This helps you appear in search results for relevant queries.

4. Add a Strategic Link

Instagram allows just one clickable link in your bio, so make it count. Use it to drive traffic to your most important resource:

- A landing page for your course or product.
- A freebie like an ebook or guide to grow your email list.
- A Linktree or similar tool if you need to share multiple links.

Include a CTA in your bio to encourage clicks, such as "Grab your free guide ↓" or "Shop our latest collection."

5. Choose Highlights That Showcase Value

Instagram Highlights are like the chapters of your profile. They allow visitors to explore your most important content at a glance. Organize them into categories that align with your brand, such as:

- **About Me**: Share your story and what you stand for.

- **Testimonials**: Showcase glowing reviews or success stories.
- **Free Resources**: Highlight tips, guides, or tutorials.
- **Products/Services**: Display what you offer and how to purchase.

Design custom covers that reflect your brand's color scheme for a polished look.

6. Post with Purpose

Your first 9–12 posts are like your shop window—what people see when they visit your profile. Make sure these posts represent your brand's best work. Include a mix of value-packed tips, engaging personal stories, and professional visuals.

Each post should align with your brand's voice and values, reinforcing why someone should hit "Follow."

7. Keep It Clean and Consistent

Finally, make sure your profile is visually cohesive. From your profile picture to your posts and highlights, everything should work together to tell a unified story.

When visitors land on your page, they should instantly understand who you are, what you do, and how you can help them. A clear, cohesive profile builds trust and sets the stage for everything else you'll achieve on Instagram.

Now that your profile is polished and purposeful, you're ready to start attracting the audience that will fuel your growth and income.

1.4 The Power of Consistency in Content

Imagine this: you walk into your favorite coffee shop, expecting the same warm atmosphere, your go-to drink, and that unmistakable aroma of freshly brewed beans. But today, it's different. The decor has changed, the menu is unrecognizable, and the barista offers a drink you've never heard of. Would you return?

This is what happens when a brand lacks consistency. People crave reliability. It builds trust, fosters connection, and sets expectations. On Instagram, consistency isn't just nice to have—it's the backbone of your content strategy.

Why Consistency Matters

Consistency on Instagram is about more than just posting regularly. It's about creating a cohesive experience across every piece of content. When done right, consistency builds your credibility and reinforces your brand identity. Here's why it's powerful:

- **Recognition**: Consistency ensures your audience recognizes your content at a glance. Whether it's your tone of voice, color palette, or style of photography, they know it's you before even reading your username.
- **Trust**: Showing up regularly proves you're dependable. Over time, your audience will come to rely on your presence, and that trust can translate into loyalty and sales.
- **Algorithm Advantage**: Instagram's algorithm favors accounts that post consistently. The more active and engaging you are, the more likely your content is to appear on feeds and explore pages.

What Consistency Looks Like

Let's break down the key areas where consistency matters most:

1. Posting Schedule

Your audience wants to know when to expect your content. You don't have to post daily, but you do need a rhythm. Whether it's three times a week or twice a day, stick to a schedule you can sustain. Tools like Later or Buffer can help you plan and automate your posts.

2. Visual Aesthetic

Your feed should feel like a unified gallery. This doesn't mean every post needs to look identical, but your colors, fonts, and style should align. For example:

- Use the same preset or filter for photos.
- Stick to a cohesive color palette.
- Ensure your fonts match your brand.

A consistent aesthetic creates a visually appealing feed that makes people want to follow and stay engaged.

3. Tone and Voice

Your captions, stories, and DMs should reflect your brand personality. Are you friendly and conversational? Inspiring and motivational? Knowledgeable and professional? Define your tone and stick to it.

4. Content Themes

Identify 3–5 core themes that align with your brand and audience's interests. For example, a personal finance account might focus on saving tips, investing, debt payoff, and financial mindset. Rotate these themes to keep your content fresh yet predictable.

How to Stay Consistent

Consistency doesn't mean perfection—it means commitment. Here's how to maintain it:

- **Batch Content**: Dedicate time to creating multiple posts in one sitting. This minimizes stress and ensures a steady flow of content.
- **Repurpose Content**: Turn a single idea into multiple formats. A popular post can become a story series, a carousel, or even a reel.
- **Plan Ahead**: Use a content calendar to map out what you'll post and when. This keeps your strategy on track and avoids last-minute scrambling.

The Results of Consistency

Consistency compounds over time. Initially, it might feel like you're shouting into the void, but stay the course. Your audience will notice your reliability, and as trust grows, so will your engagement and influence.

Chapter 2: Crafting Evergreen Content

In the fast-moving world of Instagram, trends come and go, but evergreen content remains a steady beacon of value. Unlike viral posts that flare brightly and quickly fade, evergreen content is timeless—it continues to educate, inspire, or entertain your audience long after it's published.

Crafting evergreen content isn't just a strategy; it's an investment in the longevity of your brand. By creating posts that remain relevant, you build a library of resources that keep drawing in new followers, generating engagement, and even driving sales for months or years to come.

What Is Evergreen Content?

Evergreen content addresses universal questions, needs, or desires that don't expire. It's the "how-to" guide, the timeless tips, or the motivational story that remains relevant regardless of trends or seasons.

For example:

- **Fitness Niche**: A post about "5 Beginner-Friendly Exercises You Can Do at Home" will remain useful no matter how workout fads evolve.
- **Finance Niche**: "How to Create a Budget That Works for You" will appeal to anyone starting their financial journey, whether today or two years from now.

- **Lifestyle Niche**: "10 Ways to Reduce Stress in Your Daily Life" is universally appealing, as stress management is a perennial concern.

Evergreen content doesn't have an expiration date, making it the backbone of a sustainable Instagram strategy.

The Benefits of Evergreen Content

- **Continuous Engagement**: Unlike trendy posts that fade, evergreen content continues to attract likes, comments, and shares over time.
- **Repurposing Potential**: You can revisit and repurpose evergreen content across different formats—turn a popular carousel into a video or expand it into a blog post.
- **Searchability**: If paired with the right hashtags and SEO strategies, evergreen content can surface in searches long after it's published.
- **Time Efficiency**: Once created, evergreen content keeps working for you, allowing you to focus on other growth strategies.

How to Craft Evergreen Content

1. Focus on Foundational Topics

Identify the core themes in your niche that will always be relevant. Think about the questions your audience consistently asks or the problems they need to be solved.

For instance, if you're in the wellness niche, topics like "Simple Healthy Recipes" or "The Benefits of Daily Meditation" will never go out of style.

2. Be Clear and Actionable

The best evergreen content is easy to understand and immediately useful. Break down complex ideas into digestible steps. Provide tips, tricks, or frameworks that your audience can apply right away.

3. Use High-Quality Visuals

Timeless content deserves timeless design. Choose clean, high-quality images or graphics that won't look outdated in six months. Avoid using trendy filters or fonts that might lose their appeal.

4. Write for Longevity

Avoid references to specific dates, events, or fleeting trends. Instead of saying, "This year, prioritize self-care," say, "Prioritize self-care in your daily routine." Keep your language broad and applicable to any time frame.

5. Optimize for Sharing

Evergreen content often gets shared repeatedly, so make it easy for your audience to spread the word. Create posts that inspire saving, sharing, or bookmarking, such as infographics, carousels, or mini-guides.

Examples of Evergreen Formats

- **How-To Guides**: Step-by-step instructions on solving a problem or learning a skill.
- **Lists and Tips**: Bite-sized nuggets of wisdom, such as "10 Morning Routines for Better Productivity."
- **FAQs**: Answer the most common questions in your niche.
- **Myth-Busting Posts**: Clear up misconceptions, such as "5 Myths About Investing You Should Stop Believing."
- **Inspirational Stories**: Share personal or universal stories with lessons that resonate across time.

Keeping Evergreen Content Alive

Evergreen doesn't mean static. Revisit your best-performing posts periodically to refresh captions, update visuals, or tweak hashtags. This ensures they stay relevant and continue delivering value.

For example, if your evergreen post on "Instagram Growth Tips" references outdated features, update it to include new tools or strategies.

When you master the art of evergreen content, you're not just creating posts—you're building an archive of value that keeps giving, long after the initial upload. Evergreen content is the gift that keeps on giving, for both your audience and your brand.

2.1 What Is Evergreen Content and Why It's Key to Passive Income

Imagine planting a tree that bears fruit every season without fail. You water it once, nourish it initially, and over time, it thrives independently, rewarding you with a steady harvest year after year. That's exactly what evergreen content does for your Instagram business—it's a self-sustaining asset that keeps working for you long after you've created it.

At its core, evergreen content is timeless. Unlike trend-based posts that spike in popularity but fade quickly, evergreen content remains relevant and valuable indefinitely. It answers universal questions, solves persistent problems, or provides enduring inspiration. This durability is why evergreen content is a cornerstone of passive income strategies.

What Makes Content Evergreen?

Not all posts are created equal. For content to be considered evergreen, it must meet specific criteria:

1. Timeless Appeal

Evergreen content is not tied to fleeting trends or current events. Instead, it focuses on foundational topics within your niche—ideas and solutions that stand the test of time.

For example, a post titled "How to Save Money on Groceries Without Sacrificing Quality" will be as useful five years from now as it is today. Compare that to a post about "The Top 5 Grocery Trends of 2024," which has a built-in expiration date.

2. Broad Relevance

Evergreen content appeals to a wide audience. It addresses issues or goals that are universally understood and sought after. This makes it shareable and continuously discoverable.

3. Reusable and Repurposable

Because it's not tied to a specific moment, evergreen content can be repurposed into different formats over time. A popular Instagram post might become a blog article, a carousel, or even a video tutorial.

Why Evergreen Content Drives Passive Income

The beauty of evergreen content lies in its longevity and adaptability. Here's how it contributes to your passive income goals:

1. Continuous Traffic and Engagement

Evergreen posts consistently attract new eyes to your profile. Whether someone discovers your content today or six months from now, it remains relevant and valuable, driving steady traffic to your page.

2. Lead Generation on Autopilot

Evergreen content often serves as a gateway to your offers. By embedding clear calls-to-action (CTAs) in your posts—such as downloading a free guide, enrolling in a course, or visiting your affiliate link—you create a passive funnel that converts casual viewers into paying customers.

3. Reduced Content Creation Pressure

Once your evergreen content library is built, you're no longer under constant pressure to churn out new posts. These timeless pieces keep working for you, freeing up time to focus on other aspects of your business.

4. Long-Term Affiliate Revenue

If your evergreen content incorporates affiliate links, you can generate recurring commissions without additional effort. For instance, a guide on "Essential Tools for Starting a Podcast" with affiliate links to microphones or editing software can yield steady income as readers click through and purchase.

How to Identify Evergreen Opportunities in Your Niche

Start by asking these questions:

- What questions does my audience frequently ask?
- What challenges do they face repeatedly?
- What foundational knowledge or skills are essential in my niche?

For example, if your niche is fitness, consider creating content like "10 Exercises for Beginners" or "How to Stay Consistent with Your Workouts." These topics never go out of style and cater to both newcomers and seasoned followers.

Evergreen Content in Action

Let's say you run a digital marketing page. A post titled "5 Steps to Write the Perfect Instagram Caption" fits the evergreen mold. It's actionable, universally relevant, and timeless. You include a CTA to download a free caption template, capturing email leads effortlessly. Over time, this one post generates thousands of downloads, feeding your email list with potential customers for your paid courses or services.

Building Your Evergreen Foundation

Creating evergreen content is not about quick wins—it's about strategic investments. With every piece you craft, you're building an asset that grows your brand, attracts leads, and generates passive income over time. By focusing on what lasts, you're not just creating content—you're creating wealth.

2.2 Content Types That Stand the Test of Time

Picture this: You've just spent hours crafting the perfect post, pouring your heart into the words and imagery. It goes live, and for a moment, it feels like magic. Your audience engages, likes to pour in, and your heart swells with the satisfaction of a job well done. But as the days pass, something shifts. The engagement drops. The post fades into the background as new content takes its place.

It's a scenario every content creator knows all too well—the fleeting nature of viral posts. Yet, there's another type of content, the kind that doesn't just sparkle momentarily but endures. These are the content types that stand the test of time, continuously attracting new eyes, fostering engagement, and driving long-term value. They don't just exist for a moment; they become lasting assets that work for you, even when you're not posting.

1. How-To Guides and Tutorials

One of the most powerful types of evergreen content is the how-to guide. People are always looking for ways to solve problems or learn new skills. If you can offer clear, actionable instructions on a topic within your niche, you create content that will be relevant for years to come.

For example, if you're in the fitness niche, a post like "How to Build a Home Workout Routine in 5 Easy Steps" will continue to be valuable no matter how many trends come and go. The format is simple, yet highly effective. It can be repurposed as a blog, a video tutorial, or even a downloadable resource. The key is to focus on foundational knowledge that doesn't go out of style.

2. Lists and Tips

People love lists. They're digestible, easy to read, and incredibly shareable. Whether it's a numbered list of actionable tips, a collection of essential tools, or a roundup of resources, these types of posts tend to have long-lasting appeal.

Take the example of a post titled "10 Must-Have Apps for Productivity" or "5 Simple Ways to Stay Motivated While Working from Home." These are lists that never lose their relevance. As new apps come out or new tips emerge, you can update and refresh your list, keeping it current without losing its foundational value.

Lists and tips also work well because they're packed with easily shareable nuggets of wisdom. When people find something valuable, they want to share it with their followers, expanding your reach and perpetuating the longevity of the content.

3. Frequently Asked Questions (FAQs)

FAQ posts are another gem that stands the test of time. Throughout your Instagram journey, you'll notice recurring questions from your audience. Whether it's about a specific product, service, or general advice, these questions are opportunities for you to create content that solves problems and clarifies doubts.

For example, a beauty influencer might receive questions about "How to Choose the Right Foundation for Your Skin Type" or a tech expert could answer "How to Improve Your Phone's Battery Life." These questions are timeless. People will continue asking them, and as long as you provide answers, your content will remain relevant and valuable.

Additionally, FAQ posts can be recycled into Instagram stories or video content, expanding their reach and impact across different formats.

4. Inspirational Stories and Case Studies

We all love a good story, especially one that's inspiring. Whether it's your journey, a success story from a client, or a case study that showcases the transformation your product or service brings, these posts resonate deeply.

Stories have a unique power—they connect us emotionally. They stir something inside us, whether it's hope, inspiration, or motivation. A post about how you went from zero to thriving with your Instagram business or a story about how someone used your advice to achieve their goals will continue to inspire people for years.

As long as you keep the essence of your story alive, it will resonate with future generations, allowing you to connect with new followers who can benefit from your experience.

5. Resource Roundups and Guides

A resource roundup is a collection of the best tools, apps, books, websites, or anything of value that your audience can refer to. The beauty of resource content is that it's evergreen by nature. As long as the resources remain relevant, the post stays useful.

For instance, a post titled "The Ultimate Guide to Online Learning Platforms" will be useful as long as those platforms continue to operate. These posts are also highly shareable, meaning your audience will refer back to them time and time again, driving continued traffic to your account.

Creating Content That Endures

The key to creating content that stands the test of time is to focus on value. How can you make people's lives easier, better, or more enjoyable? Answer their questions, solve their problems, and provide lasting resources they can turn to over and over again.

By mastering these content types—how-to guides, lists, FAQs, stories, and resource roundups—you create a library of content that works hard for you, generating engagement and passive income long after the initial post. This timeless content becomes the bedrock of your Instagram strategy, allowing you to scale your business without constantly chasing the next trend.

2.3 Strategies for Creating Engaging Posts, Reels, and Stories

The secret to success on Instagram isn't just posting regularly—it's about creating content that captures your audience's attention, keeps them engaged, and drives action. Whether it's a photo post, a Reel, or a Story, each type of content has its rhythm and style. Mastering these formats doesn't just help you build an engaged community—it lays the foundation for consistent passive income. So, how do you create content that resonates and keeps people coming back for more?

1. Master the Art of the Instagram Post

Instagram posts remain one of the most reliable ways to connect with your audience, share value, and build your brand's identity. But to make your posts truly engaging, there's a blend of strategy and creativity that must go into each one.

Craft Captivating Captions

Your caption is just as important as your image. It's the space where you can connect with your audience on a personal level. Don't just describe the photo—tell a story, ask a question, or share an anecdote that makes people want to engage.

For example, if you're in the wellness niche, instead of saying, "Here's a picture of my morning yoga routine," try something like, "Yoga isn't just about flexibility; it's about setting the tone for your day. What's the first thing you do to feel grounded?" This invites your followers to share their routines in the comments and start a conversation.

Call to Action (CTA)

Your posts should always prompt your audience to do something. Whether it's leaving a comment, sharing the post, or clicking a link in your bio, a strong CTA encourages interaction and amplifies engagement. Simple phrases like, "Tag a friend who needs to see this!" or "Save this for later!" work wonders.

2. Reels: The Power of Short-Form Video

Reels are Instagram's answer to TikTok's success—and they are a game-changer when it comes to engagement. With short-form videos taking center stage, Reels offer a dynamic way to showcase your personality, share behind-the-scenes moments, or highlight your products in a fun, attention-grabbing way.

Start with a Hook

The first few seconds of your Reel are crucial. If you don't capture your audience's attention immediately, they'll scroll right past. Start with a question, an exciting statement, or an intriguing visual that invites viewers to stay.

For example, if you're in the travel niche, you might begin with a quick shot of a stunning destination and a text overlay: "Want to travel for free? Here's how I did it." This hook sparks curiosity and encourages people to keep watching.

Focus on Value

Reels thrive on quick, digestible content. Offer valuable insights, tips, or entertainment in a compact format. Whether it's a "How-to" or a "Did you know?" fact, make sure every Reel you post leaves your audience with something they can take away.

Consistency Is Key

Post Reels regularly to maintain momentum. Instagram's algorithm favors frequent Reels, rewarding creators who engage consistently with the platform. The more you post, the more visibility you'll get.

3. Stories: Authentic, Real-Time Engagement

Instagram Stories are the perfect tool for showing off your personality, engaging with your audience, and sharing real-time updates. With their temporary nature, Stories allow for more authentic, behind-the-scenes content that doesn't have to be as polished as your feed posts or Reels. But how can you make sure your Stories stand out?

Use Polls, Quizzes, and Questions

Interactive features like polls, quizzes, and question stickers are designed for engagement. They not only increase your interaction rates but also give you a better understanding of your audience's preferences. Imagine sharing a beauty tip and asking, "Which product do you swear by? Vote now!" You're not just engaging them—you're learning what resonates.

Share Behind-the-Scenes Content

Your audience loves to see what's happening behind the scenes. Whether it's a peek into your creative process, a sneak preview of a new product, or a day in your life, Stories offer a chance for your followers to connect with you on a deeper level. Show them your real self—flaws, victories, and all.

Incorporate User-Generated Content

Feature your followers' posts, reviews, or testimonials. Not only does this provide social proof, but it also encourages your audience to engage more with your content, knowing they might get featured.

4. Use Hashtags Strategically

Hashtags aren't just a way to categorize your content—they're an effective tool to increase your discoverability. While it's important not to overstuff your posts with hashtags, using a mix of niche-specific, broad, and trending hashtags can help you expand your reach. Aim for a balance between hashtags with large followings and smaller, more targeted ones.

5. Track Your Results and Adjust

Creating engaging posts, Reels, and Stories is a dynamic process. What works one week may need adjusting the next. Use Instagram's insights to track what types of content generate the most engagement. Pay attention to when your audience is most active, which content gets the most likes, shares, and saves, and adjust your strategy accordingly.

Creating Engaging Content: The Takeaway

Engaging content is not just about getting likes and comments—it's about building a lasting relationship with your audience. Whether through posts, Reels, or Stories, always aim to provide value, spark conversation, and create moments that resonate. As you master the art of engagement, you'll find that your Instagram presence grows, your followers become more loyal, and your business flourishes.

2.4 Leveraging Analytics to Understand What Works

Imagine this: You've been posting consistently on Instagram, creating content that you believe will resonate with your audience, but the engagement seems to plateau. The likes are trickling in, but they're not quite as abundant as before. The comments are fewer, and your follower growth is no longer as rapid. This is where the power of Instagram's analytics comes into play—a tool that can transform your content strategy and help you uncover exactly what works.

Analytics are like a treasure map, guiding you through the terrain of your Instagram journey. By understanding the numbers, you can fine-tune your strategy and create content that not only drives engagement but also sustains long-term growth. So how do you unlock the full potential of Instagram analytics to refine your approach?

1. Understanding Key Metrics

Instagram provides a wealth of data through its Insights feature, giving you access to vital statistics that can inform every decision you make. Let's break down some of the most important metrics:

Engagement Rate

Engagement is the lifeblood of your content's success. Likes, comments, shares, and saves all contribute to your engagement rate. A higher engagement rate signals that your content is resonating with your audience. When analyzing your posts, pay attention to which ones generate the most interaction. Are they educational? Inspirational? Humorous? Identifying trends in your highest-performing posts will give you insight into the type of content your followers connect with most.

Reach and Impressions

Reach tells you how many unique accounts have seen your post, while impressions track the total number of times your post has been viewed, regardless of whether it's the same user. These numbers reveal your visibility. If your reach is high but engagement is low, it may suggest that while people are seeing your content, they're not compelled to interact. This could be a sign to revise your captions, improve your calls to action, or rework your visuals to better grab attention.

Follower Activity

When are your followers most active? Instagram provides insights into the days and times when your audience is most engaged with your content. This is crucial information for timing your posts. For example, if your followers are most active in the evenings, scheduling your posts for that time will give your content a better chance of reaching its maximum audience.

2. Interpreting Content Performance

Once you've identified key metrics, the next step is understanding what's working—and more importantly, what isn't. It's easy to become attached to certain types of content, but the analytics offer a more objective perspective.

Content Type Performance

Take note of which content types—posts, Reels, Stories, or carousels—generate the most engagement. For example, you may find that your Reels are driving more interaction than your standard posts. This insight can lead you to create more short-form videos, capitalizing on what your audience responds to most. Alternatively, if your carousels are thriving, you might want to post more educational content in that format, ensuring that your followers continue to swipe and engage.

Post Composition

Don't just look at what you post but how you post it. Which types of captions are leading to higher engagement? Is there a specific style or theme (e.g., humor, personal stories, educational content) that resonates more? Do your audience prefer posts with questions or calls to action? By testing different caption styles, you can fine-tune your approach to find the voice that appeals to your community.

3. Using Data to Optimize Content Strategy

Once you've gathered your insights, the real magic happens when you use that data to evolve your content strategy. Analytics are not a one-time check—they should be used continuously to inform decisions and optimize future posts. For example:

A/B Testing

If you're unsure about what works, try A/B testing. This involves creating two variations of the same post (for example, a different caption, image, or CTA) and comparing the performance. By testing small changes, you can learn which version your audience prefers and make data-backed decisions moving forward.

Content Calendar Adjustments

With the information about when your audience is most active, you can adjust your content calendar to ensure your posts are going live at optimal times. This simple shift can lead to an immediate boost in reach and engagement, as your content is more likely to be seen by your audience when they're actively scrolling.

Refining Your Niche

Analytics can also help refine your niche. For instance, you may discover that certain subtopics within your niche generate more interaction than others. If you're in the wellness space and find that posts about mindfulness perform better than those about fitness routines, it might be worth exploring more mindfulness-related content.

4. Staying Adaptable

Instagram is constantly evolving, and so should your strategy. New features, trends, and changes to the algorithm can impact what works on the platform. Regularly revisiting your analytics ensures that you're staying on top of shifts in user behavior. Don't be afraid to tweak your strategy based on new insights or seasonal trends—staying flexible is key to long-term success.

5. The Bigger Picture: Turning Data into Passive Income

By leveraging analytics, you're not just optimizing for engagement—you're optimizing for passive income. Whether you're selling a digital course, promoting affiliate products, or offering a service, understanding what content drives conversions is crucial. If you notice that certain posts consistently lead to clicks on your affiliate links or increase sales of your digital products, double down on creating more of that type of content.

Analytics is your roadmap to a more effective Instagram strategy. When used correctly, it allows you to stop guessing and start growing, making informed decisions that fuel the growth of your brand and your passive income.

Chapter 3: Growing and Engaging Your Audience

The allure of Instagram is undeniable. Its visual appeal, dynamic content, and reach make it a platform where dreams can be built—where your business can grow, your brand can thrive, and your influence can multiply. But there's one vital ingredient that fuels all of this: your audience. Without a loyal, engaged following, Instagram is nothing more than an empty stage. So, how do you grow and engage your audience in ways that not only expand your reach but cultivate a community of raving fans? Let's dive in.

1. Cultivate a Community, Not Just a Follower Count

It's easy to get caught up in the numbers. 10K followers. 100K followers. A million followers. But behind those digits are real people—individuals with interests, challenges, and desires. Rather than viewing your audience as mere statistics, treat them like a community. When you do this, you start to build deeper connections and relationships.

Start by responding to comments and messages. A simple acknowledgment of your followers' support can go a long way. Take the time to engage with their content too. Like their posts, comment on their stories, and be genuinely interested in what they're sharing. The more you engage with your community, the more likely they are to engage with you in return.

It's also important to remember that growing an engaged audience isn't just about attracting people—it's about retaining them. Focus on nurturing relationships with those who resonate with your content. Regularly check-in, ask for feedback, and be receptive to their needs and interests.

2. Create Content That Sparks Conversations

Engagement is a two-way street. To foster meaningful conversations, you need to create content that encourages your followers to interact. Start by asking questions that prompt responses. Instead of simply posting a picture of your product, ask, "What's your biggest challenge with [topic]?" or "How do you incorporate this into your daily routine?" This allows your followers to share their thoughts and opens the door to deeper engagement.

Polls, quizzes, and question stickers are another great way to spark conversation. These interactive features allow your followers to participate in real-time, creating a more intimate, engaging experience. For example, a fitness influencer might use a poll to ask, "Do you prefer cardio or strength training?" This simple question invites followers to weigh in, while also creating an opportunity for them to feel heard and valued.

Moreover, creating content that resonates with your audience's emotions is powerful. People love to feel seen and understood. Whether through an inspiring message, a relatable meme, or an educational post, crafting content that speaks directly to your audience's experiences will keep them coming back for more.

3. Leverage Instagram's Features for Greater Engagement

Instagram offers a variety of features designed to increase engagement. Reels, Stories, and IGTV are all tools at your disposal, each offering unique ways to capture your audience's attention. But how do you use them effectively?

Reels are an excellent way to showcase your creativity. This format gives you the chance to produce short, engaging videos that are more likely to be shared, liked, and commented on. Reels have a broad reach, so take advantage of trending sounds, hashtags, and challenges to get noticed.

Stories offer a more casual, behind-the-scenes look at your life or business. Use Stories to connect on a personal level with your audience. Post polls, behind-the-scenes content, or even "this or that" questions that encourage your followers to interact in the moment. Stories also create a sense of urgency—because they disappear after 24 hours, followers are more likely to engage right away.

Instagram Lives gives you a unique opportunity to engage with your followers in real time. Hosting a live session allows you to answer questions, discuss your niche, or feature a guest. The direct connection you establish during a live session can strengthen relationships and encourage more meaningful interactions with your audience.

By consistently leveraging these features, you increase the chances of being seen by a broader audience, which directly impacts your growth and engagement.

4. Collaborate and Network to Expand Your Reach

Growing your audience isn't just about creating content. Collaboration is one of the most powerful ways to increase your visibility and attract new followers. Partnering with influencers, brands, or even followers within your niche can expose you to an entirely new group of potential followers.

Look for opportunities to collaborate on content or promotions that benefit both parties. For example, you could host a giveaway with a fellow influencer in your niche, cross-promote each other's content, or team up for a joint Instagram Live session. These collaborations give you access to their followers, helping you grow your audience organically.

Don't forget about user-generated content (UGC). Encourage your followers to create content featuring your products or services, and repost their content on your feed. This not only builds trust with your community but also spreads the word to their followers. People love being featured, and when they are, it can create a sense of loyalty and encourage further engagement.

5. Analyze and Adapt

Growing and engaging your audience is a continuous process that requires analysis and adaptation. Use Instagram Insights to understand what types of content your audience is engaging with the most. What posts get the most comments? Which Stories have the highest view count? What time of day do your followers interact the most? Once you gather this data, adjust your content strategy accordingly.

If you find that your followers prefer educational content over inspirational quotes, lean into that. If they respond well to humor, add more lighthearted content to your feed. Adapting your content based on audience behavior ensures you're always delivering what your followers crave.

Building and engaging an Instagram audience isn't an overnight task. It takes time, consistency, and a genuine investment in your followers. By focusing on creating valuable, relatable content, fostering conversations, leveraging Instagram's features, and collaborating with others, you'll not only grow your audience but also build a loyal community that sticks with you for the long haul.

Remember, an engaged audience is more than just numbers on a screen. It's a community that supports you, shares your message, and drives the growth of your business. When you invest in your audience, they'll invest in you—and that's where the magic happens.

3.1 How to Build an Authentic Following

In the age of curated feeds and influencer marketing, the concept of building an authentic following on Instagram can sometimes seem like a lofty goal, one that's difficult to reach amidst a sea of vanity metrics and trending hashtags. But the truth is, authenticity is the key to long-term success, both for personal brands and businesses. When you build an authentic following, you're not just amassing numbers—you're cultivating a community that values what you offer and believes in your mission.

So, how do you go about attracting followers who are genuinely interested in what you do and willing to engage with you long-term? Let's break it down.

1. Stay True to Your Values and Message

The foundation of authenticity lies in staying true to who you are and what you stand for. The temptation to mimic others—especially those who seem to have found "the formula" for success—can be strong. But remember, authenticity isn't about copying trends or chasing the spotlight. It's about being unapologetically yourself.

Define your values and make sure your content consistently reflects those beliefs. Whether you're passionate about fitness, sustainable fashion, or mental health awareness, your audience should know exactly what you represent from the moment they stumble upon your profile. Consistency in your message and tone creates trust, and trust is the bedrock of any authentic following.

2. Share Your Story

People connect with stories. The raw, unfiltered truth of who you are, how you've gotten to where you are, and where you're headed next can be more captivating than a perfectly staged photo. Don't be afraid to share the ups and downs of your journey. Vulnerability breeds relatability, and it's this relatability that will attract people who see themselves in your story.

Sharing personal anecdotes, challenges you've overcome, and lessons learned show your audience that you're human, not just a brand. This authentic connection is far more powerful than any polished, promotional post. For instance, a small-business owner can share a "behind-the-scenes" look at the struggles of building their brand—this kind of content resonates more deeply than just showcasing finished products.

3. Engage with Your Audience—Genuinely

Authenticity is a two-way street. It's not just about creating content and waiting for people to flock to you; it's about building relationships. Respond to comments, answer direct messages, and engage with your audience's content as well. Ask questions, participate in conversations, and show up consistently.

The more you engage with your followers on a personal level, the more they'll feel like they are part of your journey. A thoughtful response to a comment or a meaningful conversation with a follower makes a huge impact. Remember, it's not about quantity but the quality of interactions that makes your audience feel valued.

4. Create Content That Serves Your Audience

Your followers are investing their time into you, so it's crucial that you, in turn, invest in them. One way to ensure that your following remains engaged and authentic is by creating content that is genuinely useful to them. This doesn't mean you have to be an expert in everything, but it does mean being thoughtful about what your audience values.

If you're a fitness influencer, instead of just posting workout videos, you could provide tips on healthy living, share your favorite recipes, or even host Q&A sessions where you answer common fitness questions. By providing real value, you position yourself as an authority while simultaneously giving your audience a reason to stick around.

5. Be Transparent and Honest

Transparency builds trust. Don't be afraid to show the mess behind the magic. If you've had a setback, are trying a new approach, or are experiencing growth pains, be upfront about it. Honesty creates a sense of authenticity that can't be faked.

For instance, if you're promoting a product, share why you truly believe in it—don't just sell it because it's trending or there's an affiliate commission attached. People appreciate the truth, and when they sense that you're transparent, they're more likely to stay loyal.

6. Collaborate with Like-Minded Influencers

Building an authentic following doesn't always mean going it alone. Collaborating with others who share your values and vision can significantly expand your reach. These partnerships allow you to tap into a new audience while still staying true to your brand's identity. But be mindful—authenticity is key here too. Only collaborate with people whose values align with yours.

For example, if you are passionate about eco-friendly living, collaborating with a fellow influencer who promotes sustainable practices will feel more natural and genuine to both of your audiences. This fosters an environment where the collaboration feels authentic rather than transactional.

7. Be Patient and Persistent

Building an authentic following doesn't happen overnight. It's a slow burn, not a sprint. There will be moments of frustration, especially when it feels like your follower count isn't rising as quickly as you'd hoped. But remember: authenticity doesn't thrive on shortcuts. Stay consistent with your message, keep engaging with your community, and be patient with the process.

The followers who come to you naturally—those who resonate with your story and your values—are the ones who will stay. And over time, this loyal base will become your biggest advocates, helping you grow in ways that feel real, meaningful, and lasting.

Building an authentic following is not about seeking validation or chasing the next viral trend. It's about forging real, meaningful connections with people who resonate with you, your values, and your message. Authenticity takes time and effort, but the rewards are worth it. When you build an audience that believes in you and what you stand for, you create not just followers—but lifelong supporters who will grow with you.

In a world full of noise, being true to yourself is your most powerful tool. And remember: the most authentic part of your brand is you.

3.2 Mastering Instagram's Algorithm: Tips for Visibility

When it comes to growing your presence on Instagram, understanding the algorithm is not just helpful—it's essential. Instagram's algorithm is a complex beast, constantly evolving to provide the best experience for its users. The challenge for creators and businesses is to make sure their content gets the visibility it deserves, even when the odds seem stacked against them. But fear not: with the right strategy, you can work with the algorithm, not against it, and watch your engagement soar.

So, how do you master the algorithm to increase your visibility? Let's dive into the key factors that influence how Instagram's algorithm works, and how you can optimize your content for maximum exposure.

1. Engagement Is Everything

Instagram's algorithm thrives on engagement, and it rewards content that gets people interacting. Whether it's liking, commenting, sharing, or saving, the more engagement your posts receive, the more likely they are to be shown to a broader audience. Think of engagement as the fuel that powers your content's journey to new eyes.

So, how do you get engagement?

First, ask your audience to engage! Craft captions that encourage people to share their thoughts, opinions, or experiences. Use questions, polls, and call-to-action phrases like, "Tag a friend who would love this!" or "Which one is your favorite—1, 2, or 3?" The more engaged your followers are, the more Instagram's algorithm will notice—and push your content out.

Second, respond to your followers. Instagram rewards interaction. By replying to comments, liking their posts, and engaging in meaningful conversations, you'll increase the chances of your content showing up on their feeds. And remember: engagement isn't just a one-way street—get involved in conversations with other creators and audiences as well.

2. Prioritize Quality Over Quantity

Gone are the days when posting multiple times a day was the surefire path to Instagram success. Now, it's about posting quality content that resonates with your audience, not simply hitting the "publish" button for the sake of it. The algorithm now places a higher value on content that encourages meaningful interactions and sparks interest.

Instead of posting just to post, focus on creating high-quality, thoughtful content that your followers can relate to. Whether it's a well-crafted caption, stunning visuals, or engaging videos, make sure that your content provides value. When you produce content that makes people stop scrolling, you create an opportunity for engagement, and ultimately, for Instagram to recognize your posts as high-value content.

3. Consistency is Key

While quality reigns supreme, consistency remains a vital part of your Instagram strategy. The algorithm favors accounts that consistently post valuable content because it indicates that you're active and invested in the platform. But consistency doesn't just mean frequent posting; it's about creating a steady stream of content that aligns with your brand and engages your audience.

Find a rhythm that works for you, whether it's posting once a day or three times a week. Make sure you're consistently offering your followers something they can look forward to, whether that's educational content, behind-the-scenes glimpses, or entertaining stories. The more consistently you show up, the more the algorithm will favor your posts.

4. Leverage Reels and Stories

Instagram has been heavily promoting Reels and Stories, which means they're the content types that the algorithm is currently rewarding most. Reels, in particular, are a great way to increase your reach, especially because they're featured in a separate section of Instagram, making them discoverable to a larger audience.

Don't be afraid to get creative with your Reels—use trending sounds, add eye-catching visuals, and incorporate humor or educational elements that reflect your brand. Similarly, Stories are a powerful tool to connect with your followers on a more personal level. Use interactive features like polls, questions, and quizzes to keep your audience engaged and involved in your content.

Both Reels and Stories give you a chance to showcase a different side of your brand, making your content feel more well-rounded and engaging. Plus, they help you stay at the forefront of your followers' minds.

5. The Power of Hashtags

Hashtags still play a key role in helping your content get discovered. The right hashtags can put your posts in front of users who are interested in your niche but may not be following you yet. Research the best hashtags for your audience and industry, but don't just rely on the popular ones.

Instagram's algorithm also rewards niche and specific hashtags, as they help Instagram understand what your content is about. Combine a mix of broad, high-volume hashtags and niche-specific ones to increase your chances of reaching a targeted audience.

Be mindful of how many hashtags you use. While Instagram allows you to add up to 30, studies suggest that between 5 and 10 hashtags are optimal for boosting engagement. Experiment with different combinations and analyze which hashtags work best for your posts.

6. Post When Your Audience Is Active

Timing matters. Posting when your followers are most active increases the chances that your content will be seen and engaged with right away, which sends a signal to Instagram that your post is valuable and worth showing to more people.

Use Instagram Insights (available for business accounts) to understand when your followers are online and make sure you're posting during peak hours. Typically, early mornings and evenings are great times to post, but your audience's habits may vary. Pay attention to the trends in your Insights and adjust your posting schedule accordingly.

7. Don't Forget About Video Content

The algorithm favors video content because it tends to keep users engaged longer. The more time people spend watching your video content, the more likely Instagram is to recommend it to others. So, whether you're posting an IGTV, Reel, or a simple video in your feed, keep your videos interesting, informative, and entertaining to encourage longer view times.

While Instagram's algorithm may seem mysterious and ever-changing, the truth is that it's designed to reward content that is engaging, relevant, and valuable to its users. The key is to align your content strategy with these priorities and focus on creating quality, authentic content that resonates with your audience. Engage consistently, post valuable content, and keep an eye on trends like Reels and Stories.

By understanding and working with the algorithm, not against it, you'll increase your visibility, grow your audience, and create meaningful connections that will fuel your Instagram success.

3.3 Creating Community Through Interaction and Engagement

In a world where followers are often seen as just numbers, one of the most powerful assets you can build on Instagram is a thriving, engaged community. A community is more than just a collection of people who follow you; it's a group of individuals who feel connected to you, your content, and, most importantly, each other. This is where the true influence lies—the ability to create a space where your audience feels seen, heard, and valued.

Building a community takes time, effort, and authenticity, but the rewards are immense. A loyal, engaged community doesn't just increase your visibility—it fuels your growth and drives the long-term success of your brand. So, how do you create such a community on Instagram? It all boils down to interaction and engagement.

1. Foster Two-Way Conversations

Engagement on Instagram isn't just about posting content and hoping people interact with it. It's about opening the door for conversations and then actively participating in them. The key to building a community lies in the interaction you create with your followers. If you want your audience to feel involved, you have to show up for them. Respond to comments, reply to DMs, and, most importantly, make your followers feel that their voice matters.

Take a moment to reflect on your own experiences as a user of Instagram. The accounts you engage with the most are likely those that respond to your comments or acknowledge your messages. Now, imagine the power you could harness if you took the time to respond to every meaningful comment and message your audience leaves. It shows that you value their engagement and that you are building a space where dialogue is not just encouraged—it's expected.

2. Be Authentic and Relatable

Authenticity is at the heart of any thriving community. People want to connect with real people, not faceless brands or accounts that feel distant.

Share your personal story, show behind-the-scenes moments, and don't be afraid to be vulnerable. When your followers can see the person behind the account, they'll feel a deeper connection to your content.

In addition to personal stories, relate your content to the lives of your followers. Make them feel like they are part of the conversation, not just spectators. For example, share tips and advice that your followers can implement in their own lives. Celebrate their wins and offer support when they struggle. This isn't just about posting content; it's about making your followers feel that they are part of something bigger.

3. Use Interactive Features to Spark Engagement

Instagram offers a variety of interactive features designed to boost engagement, such as polls, questions, quizzes, and sliders. These tools are perfect for sparking conversations and getting real-time feedback from your followers. By using them in your Stories or posts, you invite your audience to interact directly with your content.

But it's not enough to just use these tools—you have to follow up. If you ask your followers what their favorite product is, for example, make sure to respond with your own opinion, share the results, or even take their recommendations to heart. These small gestures show that you're listening, and they encourage people to continue engaging with you.

4. Host Live Sessions to Strengthen Bonds

Instagram Live is one of the most powerful ways to connect with your audience in real time. Live sessions create an immediate sense of connection because your followers can see and hear you directly, and they can ask questions or comment while you're on air. This level of interaction is unmatched by any other feature on the platform.

Use Instagram Live to host Q&A sessions, share exclusive content, or have casual conversations with your followers. The key is to make these sessions feel personal and authentic. Don't script your lives or make them overly polished; let your personality shine through. The more real and relatable you are, the more your followers will feel a sense of belonging within your community.

5. Celebrate Your Community

Acknowledging and celebrating your community is an essential part of making your followers feel valued. Whether it's by reposting user-generated content, running shout-out campaigns, or simply thanking your audience for their support, small gestures of recognition go a long way.

Feature your followers in your stories or posts when they engage with your content. Reposting their content not only builds goodwill but also reinforces the sense of community. When you show your followers that you appreciate them, you create a positive feedback loop that encourages even more engagement.

6. Create a Safe Space

A successful community is one that feels safe and inclusive for everyone involved. Make sure that your space is welcoming and that you establish clear guidelines for respectful behavior. Set the tone for how people should treat one another by modeling kindness, inclusivity, and authenticity in your posts and interactions.

This is especially important in a digital space where negativity can sometimes thrive. Encourage positive conversations, avoid drama, and step in when necessary to maintain a respectful environment. When people feel safe and supported, they'll return to your page time and time again, strengthening the sense of community.

7. Consistency and Presence Matter

Creating a community isn't something that happens overnight, and it's not something that can be left on the sidelines. It takes ongoing effort and consistent interaction. Show up for your followers, regularly post valuable content, and keep the conversation going. The more present you are in your community, the more likely it is to grow and thrive.

Make sure your content reflects the values and interests of your community. Create a content strategy that prioritizes their needs and desires. This shows your audience that you are fully invested in them, not just in growing your follower count.

At the core of Instagram's power lies its ability to connect people. And when you foster a community, you unlock a level of connection that goes beyond just numbers. By focusing on interaction, authenticity, and engagement, you can build a community that supports you, trusts you, and shares your content with others. This isn't just about gaining followers—it's about creating a space where people feel valued, heard, and part of something meaningful.

With patience, consistency, and genuine interaction, you'll not only grow your audience—you'll build a loyal community that will champion your brand for years to come.

3.4 Turning Followers into Loyal Fans

In the ever-evolving world of Instagram, where algorithms shift and trends come and go, there is one constant that remains invaluable: loyal fans. These are the people who don't just follow you—they believe in you, your message, and your vision. Loyal fans are the bedrock of a successful Instagram presence, transforming your account from a passive collection of followers into a thriving, engaged community. But how do you go from simply having followers to creating a tribe of loyal, passionate fans who will champion your brand and share your message with the world?

It all starts with building deep, meaningful relationships.

1. Create a Connection Through Storytelling

One of the most powerful ways to turn followers into loyal fans is through storytelling. People connect with stories on a deeply emotional level. They don't just want to see photos or read captions—they want to hear your story, understand your journey, and see themselves in it. Whether you're sharing your personal experiences, the lessons you've learned, or the values that guide your work, storytelling gives your audience something to relate to.

Consider this: why do we follow our favorite celebrities, influencers, or brands? It's because we feel a connection to them—through their stories. So, make your followers feel that connection by being open and authentic. Share the highs and the lows, the struggles and the successes, the moments that define you. When your audience feels like they're part of your journey, they become more invested in your success. And that investment transforms followers into loyal fans.

2. Consistently Provide Value

To turn a casual follower into a die-hard fan, you need to offer more than just aesthetically pleasing photos. You need to provide consistent value. What can your followers gain from being part of your community? Whether it's practical tips, emotional support, or entertainment, value is what keeps people coming back.

This value doesn't have to be grandiose. It could be as simple as offering tips that solve common problems in your niche, sharing resources that benefit your followers, or creating content that makes them smile. People appreciate knowing that when they engage with your content, they're beyond just numbers. By focusing on interaction, authenticity, and engagement, you can build a community that supports you, trusts you, and shares your content with others. This isn't just about gaining followers—it's about creating a space where people feel valued, heard, and part of something meaningful.

With patience, consistency, and genuine interaction, you'll not only grow your audience—you'll build a loyal community that will champion your brand for years to come.

3.4 Turning Followers into Loyal Fans

In the ever-evolving world of Instagram, where algorithms shift and trends come and go, there is one constant that remains invaluable: loyal fans. These are the people who don't just follow you—they believe in you, your message, and your vision. Loyal fans are the bedrock of a successful Instagram presence, transforming your account from a passive collection of followers into a thriving, engaged community. But how do you go from simply having followers to creating a tribe of loyal, passionate fans who will champion your brand and share your message with the world?

It all starts with building deep, meaningful relationships.

1. Create a Connection Through Storytelling

One of the most powerful ways to turn followers into loyal fans is through storytelling. People connect with stories on a deeply emotional level. They don't just want to see photos or read captions—they want to hear your story, understand your journey, and see themselves in it. Whether you're sharing your personal experiences, the lessons you've learned, or the values that guide your work, storytelling gives your audience something to relate to.

Consider this: why do we follow our favorite celebrities, influencers, or brands? It's because we feel a connection to them—through their stories. So, make your followers feel that connection by being open and authentic. Share the highs and the lows, the struggles and the successes, the moments that define you. When your audience feels like they're part of your journey, they become more invested in your success. And that investment transforms followers into loyal fans.

2. Consistently Provide Value

To turn a casual follower into a die-hard fan, you need to offer more than just aesthetically pleasing photos. You need to provide consistent value. What can your followers gain from being part of your community? Whether it's practical tips, emotional support, or entertainment, value is what keeps people coming back.

This value doesn't have to be grandiose. It could be as simple as offering tips that solve common problems in your niche, sharing resources that benefit your followers, or creating content that makes them smile. People appreciate knowing that when they engage with your content, they're getting something meaningful in return. When you consistently meet their needs, your followers will feel that they have a reason to stick around—and that's when you begin to turn them into loyal fans.

3. Be Present and Accessible

Loyal fans don't just exist in the digital world—they thrive in the spaces where you actively engage with them. Showing up consistently in your followers' feeds, answering their comments, liking their posts, and initiating conversations are all ways of creating that sense of presence. But it doesn't stop at the comments section.

You also need to make your followers feel that you're accessible. Instagram stories, polls, and live Q&A sessions allow you to interact with your audience in real-time, creating a two-way connection. People love feeling like they're talking to a real person, not just a brand. By being present and approachable, you build a rapport that fosters loyalty. Your followers become fans because they know you see them, hear them, and genuinely care about their experience.

4. Make Them Part of Your Story

The shift from follower to loyal fan occurs when people feel that they are part of something bigger than just following an account. You can facilitate this by creating opportunities for your audience to participate in your journey. Whether it's through user-generated content, shoutouts, or involving them in decision-making processes (like voting on a new product design or the next topic for a post), people want to feel that they're an integral part of your story.

Encourage your followers to share their own experiences, thoughts, and creations that relate to your brand. When you share their content or acknowledge their contributions, it reinforces the idea that your community is a collaboration—a place where every person matters. This sense of belonging is the spark that ignites fan loyalty.

5. Reward Loyalty with Exclusive Offers

One of the best ways to strengthen the bond between you and your followers is by rewarding their loyalty. Offer your most dedicated fans special perks, whether that's exclusive content, discounts, early access to new products, or shoutouts. This not only makes your followers feel appreciated but also incentivizes them to continue engaging with your content.

A fan who feels valued will continue to support you, engage with your posts, and spread the word to others. This can create a cycle of growth, as your loyal fans bring in new followers who eventually become loyal fans themselves.

6. Maintain Consistency and Integrity

Fans are drawn to accounts that are consistent in both their content and their values. The more you maintain a strong, unwavering presence on Instagram, the more you build trust with your audience. Loyal fans appreciate predictability—knowing they can count on you for quality content, reliable interactions, and a message that aligns with their beliefs.

Your integrity is just as important as your consistency. Fans need to trust that you stand behind your words, actions, and brand. Be transparent with your audience, and never compromise your values for the sake of growth or profit. When you stay true to who you are, your followers will remain loyal, not because of what you offer, but because they believe in what you represent.

7. Stay Engaged Even When Growth Slows

A common misconception is that turning followers into loyal fans happens quickly, especially when your account is growing rapidly. But fan loyalty is cultivated over time. There will be periods when growth slows, or when you experience dips in engagement. In these moments, your commitment to your audience is tested.

Rather than focusing on the numbers, stay engaged with your current community. Keep nurturing the relationships you've built, respond to comments, ask for feedback, and provide fresh value. Your true fans will appreciate your consistency, and this loyalty will be what carries your brand through periods of stagnation and helps it continue growing.

Turning followers into loyal fans is not an overnight process—it requires time, effort, and a deep commitment to your community. It's about building trust, providing value, and showing up authentically for your audience. When you create that strong emotional connection, your followers become more than just numbers—they become your brand's greatest advocates.

In the end, loyal fans are the ones who will help sustain your Instagram success long after the trends have passed. They'll be there through the highs and the lows, cheering you on, supporting your ventures, and helping your brand thrive in ways that go beyond mere likes and follow. Build these relationships, and your Instagram presence will grow into something far more powerful: a community that will support you for years to come.

Chapter 4: Monetizing Through Digital Courses

In the age of digital transformation, education has moved from traditional classrooms to the palm of our hands. Social media platforms, particularly Instagram, have become powerful tools not just for connection and inspiration, but for turning knowledge into profit. Among the many revenue streams available to content creators, digital courses stand out as a remarkable opportunity to monetize expertise and deliver immense value. But how do you leverage your Instagram presence to craft and sell a course that resonates with your audience? This chapter will explore the essential steps to create, promote, and profit from your own digital course.

1. Recognize Your Expertise and Niche

Before diving into the mechanics of course creation, it's essential to start with a clear understanding of what you can offer. Think about the areas where you excel, the problems your audience faces, and the expertise you've built over time. Your Instagram followers are already there because they resonate with what you share, whether that's fitness tips, business strategies, cooking hacks, or lifestyle insights.

To create a successful course, it's vital to pinpoint your niche. Ask yourself: What knowledge or skill can I teach that will genuinely benefit my followers? For instance, if you have a knack for photography, consider offering a course on mastering Instagram photography. If you're a business coach, develop a course on building a personal brand. By offering solutions to specific problems, you position your course as both valuable and unique.

2. Build a Curriculum with Purpose and Clarity

Now that you've identified your area of expertise, it's time to organize your thoughts into a structured curriculum. A well-organized course provides value through clear, actionable lessons. Each module should guide your students from point A to point B, helping them achieve specific outcomes.

Start by breaking down your course into digestible topics. For example, if your course is about Instagram marketing, you might have modules like:

- Module 1: Understanding the Instagram Algorithm

- Module 2: Content Creation Strategies
- Module 3: Engaging Your Audience Effectively
- Module 4: Monetizing Instagram for Long-Term Success

By creating a roadmap of topics, you give your students a sense of progress and achievement, motivating them to continue learning. Remember, clarity and purpose are key. Avoid overwhelming your audience with too much information; instead, focus on delivering high-value content that's easy to digest and apply.

3. Choose the Right Platform for Course Delivery

Once you've mapped out your curriculum, the next step is choosing the right platform to host and deliver your course. Thankfully, there are many tools available that make it easy to launch your course without needing to be tech-savvy. Platforms like Teachable, Thinkific, and Kajabi allow you to upload your content, design your course page, and set up payment systems—all in one place.

When choosing your platform, consider ease of use, customization options, and scalability. Your course should be easy to navigate and visually appealing, aligning with the aesthetic of your Instagram brand. Ensure that the platform you choose offers features like video hosting, quizzes, and email automation to make your course as interactive and engaging as possible.

4. Use Instagram to Promote and Build Anticipation

Once your course is ready, Instagram becomes your most valuable tool for promotion. Use your existing followers to create a buzz about your upcoming course. Start by teasing your course content in your stories and posts, offering sneak peeks or behind-the-scenes glimpses. Engage your audience by asking questions and conducting polls to spark curiosity.

When launching your course, consider using Instagram's shopping feature or a "Link in Bio" to drive traffic directly to your course page. To boost excitement, offer early bird discounts, bonuses, or exclusive access to the first few sign-ups. Be sure to use compelling visuals, share testimonials from beta testers, and showcase the benefits of the course to encourage followers to take action.

Remember, Instagram is a visual platform, so use captivating imagery, videos, and stories to create urgency and desire. Testimonials and success stories from your followers or previous students can be incredibly persuasive in convincing others to join.

5. Engage and Support Your Students

The key to maintaining loyal fans—and encouraging repeat business—is offering unparalleled support to your students. Even after the sale, it's essential to engage with your course participants, answering their questions, encouraging, and gathering feedback for improvement. This ongoing support builds trust and enhances the value of your course.

Leverage Instagram to create a community around your course. For example, you could create a private Facebook group or use Instagram's Direct Messages to keep students motivated and connected. By nurturing these relationships, you increase the likelihood of students recommending your course to others, leading to more organic growth and sales.

6. Diversify Your Offerings for Long-Term Profit

While a single course can be a lucrative income stream, the real power comes in scaling your digital education empire. Once you've built a following around one course, consider diversifying your offerings. Perhaps you can create advanced courses, offer coaching services, or even develop digital products such as e-books, workbooks, or templates.

Consider also creating a subscription model where students pay for ongoing content or exclusive access. This model allows you to build long-term passive income by continuing to offer value without constantly needing to create new material from scratch.

Monetizing your Instagram presence through digital courses isn't just about making money—it's about creating meaningful, educational experiences that resonate with your audience. By offering valuable content that solves real problems, building anticipation, and engaging with your community, you can transform your Instagram followers into loyal customers who trust your expertise.

Remember, successful course creation requires both expertise and empathy. Understand your audience's pain points, provide actionable solutions, and foster an ongoing relationship that keeps them coming back for more. By following these principles, your digital courses will not only generate income—they'll help you establish yourself as a thought leader in your niche, turning your passion into a thriving online business.

4.1 Identifying Problems Your Audience Wants Solved

At the heart of every successful digital course lies one simple truth: it solves a problem. Whether it's teaching someone how to bake the perfect sourdough loaf or how to master Instagram marketing, people invest in courses because they need help. Identifying those problems—the ones your audience truly wants to be solved—is the foundation of creating a course that sells and changes lives.

But here's the catch: many creators assume they know their audience's needs. They think, "If I struggled with this, surely others will too." While this may sometimes be true, relying solely on assumptions is a recipe for missed opportunities and lukewarm results. To craft a course that resonates, you must uncover your audience's real pain points—straight from the source.

Start by Listening: Tuning Into Your Audience's Voice

Your audience constantly tells you what they need—you just need to know where to look. Social media, particularly Instagram, is a goldmine of insights. Start by examining the comments and messages you receive. Are there recurring questions or challenges that followers mention? If you're a fitness coach, you might notice followers repeatedly asking for help with meal prep or workout motivation. If you're in fashion, they might seek advice on styling a capsule wardrobe.

Instagram Stories offer another opportunity for direct feedback. Use interactive tools like polls, question boxes, and quizzes to ask your audience what they're struggling with. For instance, if you're a financial expert, post a Story asking, "What's your biggest challenge with budgeting?" Not only will you get valuable responses, but you'll also show your followers that you care about their needs.

Analyzing Trends and Engagement

Beyond direct feedback, your existing content can reveal what resonates most. Dive into your Instagram analytics to identify posts, Reels, and Stories with the highest engagement. Look for patterns: Are your followers drawn to certain topics? Do they save or share specific posts more than others? These trends often indicate areas where your audience finds value—and where their challenges may lie.

For example, if your Reel about quick weeknight dinners went viral, it might suggest your followers struggle with finding time to cook. This insight can be the seed for a course like "30-Minute Meals for Busy Weeknights."

Understand Their Pain Points Deeply

Once you've identified potential problems, it's time to dig deeper. A surface-level understanding isn't enough; you need to get to the root of their struggles. For instance, if followers say they have trouble staying consistent with workouts, ask yourself why. Is it a lack of time? Motivation? Knowledge about what exercises to do? By understanding the underlying issues, you can create a course that addresses them head-on.

One way to uncover these insights is through one-on-one conversations. Invite a handful of your most engaged followers to hop on a quick Zoom call or chat over Instagram DMs. Frame it as an opportunity to shape future content and courses. People are often eager to share their thoughts when they feel heard.

Test Your Ideas Before You Build

Before you pour hours into creating a course, test your ideas to ensure they align with your audience's desires. Create a free or low-cost resource—a downloadable guide, a mini-challenge, or a webinar—that addresses a specific problem. Promote it on Instagram and monitor the response. A high sign-up rate signals that you've hit a nerve. For example, if your free guide on managing stress during the holidays attracts hundreds of downloads, you know there's a demand for a deeper dive into stress management.

Position Yourself as the Solution

Identifying problems is only half the battle. To truly connect with your audience, you must position yourself as the person uniquely equipped to solve them. Share your own experiences and challenges to build trust and relatability. For instance, if you're a productivity coach, talk about how you once struggled with procrastination and the steps you took to overcome it. By framing yourself as both an expert and someone who understands their pain, you'll inspire confidence in your course.

Identifying your audience's problems isn't just about creating a course that sells—it's about showing your followers that you're attuned to their needs and invested in their success. By listening to their challenges, analyzing trends, and testing ideas, you can create a course that feels tailor-made for them. Remember, the better you understand their struggles, the more impactful—and profitable—your solution will be.

4.2 Designing a High-Value Digital Course

Creating a digital course is more than compiling information; it's about crafting an experience that transforms lives. A high-value course doesn't just teach—it delivers actionable insights, practical tools, and confidence to achieve real results. Whether your course is about mastering Instagram, baking artisan bread, or achieving financial freedom, the value lies in how effectively you address your audience's needs and guide them toward their goals.

Here's how to design a course that exceeds expectations and ensures your audience sees it as worth every penny.

Step 1: Define the Transformation

Every high-value course starts with a clear transformation. Ask yourself: What will my students achieve by the end of this course? The transformation is the promise you're making to your audience. It's what motivates them to enroll and stick with the material.

For instance, if you're a fitness coach, your course's transformation might be: "By the end of this course, you'll build a sustainable workout routine that fits into your busy schedule." If you're a graphic designer, it could be: "You'll master Adobe Illustrator and create professional-grade designs." A clear transformation acts as a compass for both you and your students, ensuring every module serves a purpose.

Step 2: Map Out the Journey

Once you've defined the transformation, break it down into actionable steps. This becomes the foundation of your course structure. Each module should focus on one step, building logically toward the desired outcome.

For example, let's say your course teaches Instagram growth. Your modules might include:

- **Laying the Foundation**: Optimizing your profile and defining your brand.
- **Content Creation**: Designing posts, Reels, and Stories that attract attention.
- **Audience Engagement**: Building relationships with followers to drive loyalty.
- **Analytics Mastery**: Understanding metrics to refine your strategy.

Each module should address a specific challenge or milestone, creating a seamless journey for your students.

Step 3: Prioritize Actionable Content

Information alone doesn't create value—implementation does. High-value courses provide not only the what but also the how. This means including exercises, templates, checklists, and real-world examples that help students apply what they've learned.

For instance, instead of merely explaining Instagram hashtags, provide a worksheet for brainstorming niche-relevant tags. If your course is about cooking, include downloadable shopping lists and step-by-step video tutorials. Tangible takeaways make your course feel practical and worth the investment.

Step 4: Engage Through Multi-Modal Learning

Different people learn in different ways, so it's essential to design your course with varied formats to maximize engagement. Combine videos, PDFs, quizzes, and live Q&A sessions to cater to different learning preferences.

For example:

- **Videos**: Perfect for demonstrating complex concepts or creating a personal connection.
- **Worksheets**: Encourage hands-on learning and application.
- **Quizzes**: Reinforce key lessons and keep students accountable.
- **Live Sessions**: Offer opportunities for real-time interaction and deeper insights.

By diversifying your content, you not only enhance the learning experience but also keep students motivated.

Step 5: Include a Support System

A truly valuable course offers support beyond the core material. Consider adding a community element, such as a private Facebook group or Discord channel, where students can connect, ask questions, and celebrate wins. Alternatively, schedule live office hours where you can address common challenges and provide personalized guidance.

This additional layer of support can be the difference between a student giving up halfway through and completing your course with rave reviews.

Step 6: Test and Refine

Before launching your course, test it with a small group of beta students. This pilot group will help you identify any gaps, confusing sections, or opportunities for improvement. Encourage honest feedback and use it to refine your content.

For example, if beta testers find Module 3 too dense, break it into smaller lessons. If they struggle with implementing a concept, add an extra resource or tutorial. Continuous refinement ensures your course meets the highest standards.

Designing a high-value digital course is a labor of love. It requires empathy, attention to detail, and a commitment to delivering excellence. By focusing on transformation, creating actionable content, and supporting your students every step of the way, you'll craft a course that not only sells but also creates a lasting impact—turning your knowledge into a powerful tool for change.

4.3 Tools and Platforms for Hosting and Selling Courses

The internet is brimming with tools and platforms designed to simplify the process of hosting and selling your digital course. But here's the secret: the right choice for you depends on your goals, technical expertise, and the experience you want to deliver to your students. In this chapter, we'll explore the best options for creating a seamless course experience, ensuring that your audience remains engaged and your business thrives.

Step 1: Choosing the Right Hosting Platform

Hosting platforms are the backbone of your digital course. They provide the infrastructure for delivering your content, tracking student progress, and managing payments. Here are some of the top options to consider:

Teachable

Teachable is perfect for beginners and seasoned course creators alike. It offers an intuitive interface, customizable templates, and built-in payment gateways. Its analytics tools allow you to track student engagement, while features like quizzes and certificates keep learners motivated.

Kajabi

Kajabi is an all-in-one platform that combines course hosting with marketing automation. Beyond hosting your course, Kajabi lets you build a website, create email funnels, and manage a membership site. Its higher price point is justified by the range of tools it offers.

Thinkific

Thinkific is another user-friendly option that excels in customization. You can create visually appealing course pages, host live sessions, and integrate third-party tools. Thinkific is particularly well-suited for creators who want to maintain a professional and polished brand.

Podia

Podia stands out for its simplicity and affordability. It supports course hosting, digital downloads, webinars, and even affiliate programs. Podia's minimalist approach makes it ideal for creators who value ease of use.

Step 2: Adding Tools for Engaging Content Delivery

Once you've chosen a platform, it's time to enhance your course with engaging content delivery tools. Consider these options:

- **Loom and Camtasia** for creating high-quality video lessons. These tools are intuitive and allow you to record your screen, voice, and webcam.
- **Canva** for designing visually stunning PDFs, workbooks, and slides to complement your course material.
- **Google Forms** or **Typeform** for creating surveys, feedback forms, or quizzes to track student progress and gather insights.
- **Zoom** for hosting live Q&A sessions or workshops. Pairing live interactions with pre-recorded content fosters a stronger connection with your students.

Step 3: Streamlining the Sales Process

Your course's success depends on how easily your audience can find, purchase, and access it. Here's how to streamline the sales process:

- **Payment Gateways**: Most platforms integrate with PayPal, Stripe, or both, allowing you to offer secure transactions. Choose a gateway that supports multiple currencies to cater to a global audience.
- **Sales Funnels**: Tools like ClickFunnels or ConvertKit enable you to build email sequences and landing pages that guide potential students toward enrollment.
- **Affiliate Marketing Programs**: Many hosting platforms support affiliate programs, letting satisfied students or influencers promote your course for a commission.

Step 4: Delivering an Exceptional User Experience

A smooth user experience is non-negotiable. Choose a platform that offers mobile-friendly access, intuitive navigation, and reliable customer support. Test your course from the perspective of a student, ensuring everything from login to lesson completion works seamlessly.

The tools and platforms you choose can make or break your digital course's success. By investing in intuitive, reliable solutions and prioritizing your students' experience, you're not just hosting a course—you're creating a transformative journey. With the right infrastructure in place, your course becomes more than a product; it becomes a gateway to impact, income, and growth.

4.4 Marketing Strategies to Sell Without Feeling "Salesy"

Selling can feel like an intimidating dance, one where too much enthusiasm risks alienating your audience, while too little passion leaves your offers unnoticed. The secret to successful marketing lies in striking the perfect balance—an approach that feels authentic aligns with your values, and genuinely serves your audience. In this chapter, we'll explore marketing strategies that help you sell your digital courses effortlessly, without the heavy-handedness that turns people away.

Step 1: Shift from Selling to Serving

The first and most important mindset shift is to focus on service, not sales. People are naturally resistant to being sold to, but they're receptive to solutions that address their needs and aspirations. When you approach marketing as an opportunity to help others, it transforms the entire process into something rewarding rather than uncomfortable.

Start by asking yourself these questions:

- What specific problem does my course solve?
- How will it improve the lives of my audience?
- What frustrations, fears, or desires does it address?

When you tailor your marketing message around the value your course provides, you build trust. This trust forms the foundation for an authentic relationship where your audience feels empowered to invest in your solution.

Step 2: Storytelling as a Sales Tool

Humans are hardwired to connect with stories. Instead of leading with features or technical details about your course, share a narrative that resonates with your audience.

For example, you might start with your own journey:

- How did you overcome the challenge your course now addresses?
- What was your turning point, and how did the knowledge you're offering transform your life?

Or you can tell the stories of others:

- Highlight testimonials or success stories from beta testers or clients.
- Share relatable anecdotes that illustrate the need for your course.

By weaving storytelling into your marketing, you engage emotions, making your message more memorable and meaningful.

Step 3: Educate to Attract

One of the most effective ways to market without being pushy is to offer value upfront. By educating your audience, you position yourself as a trusted authority while simultaneously showcasing your expertise.

Here's how to do it:

- **Content Marketing**: Create blog posts, videos, or social media posts that address the pain points your course solves. For example, if your course is about Instagram growth, share tips on optimizing a profile or crafting engaging captions.
- **Free Resources**: Offer downloadable guides, webinars, or mini-courses that give a taste of what your full program delivers.
- **Live Q&A Sessions**: Host live sessions where you answer questions and subtly introduce your course as a deeper solution.

This strategy builds goodwill and allows potential buyers to experience your teaching style, increasing their confidence in your product.

Step 4: The Power of Social Proof

Nothing sells like evidence that your course works. Social proof validates your expertise and reassures hesitant buyers that they're making a sound decision.

To build compelling social proof:

- Highlight testimonials from satisfied students. Include specific results or transformations they've achieved.
- Share screenshots of positive feedback from your audience on social media or via email.
- Collaborate with influencers or industry experts who can endorse your course to their followers.

Don't underestimate the subtle power of numbers, too. Statements like "Join over 1,000 students who've transformed their Instagram presence" or "Rated 5 stars by 95% of participants" add credibility to your offer.

Step 5: Create Urgency and Scarcity

Urgency and scarcity are powerful motivators when used authentically. They encourage your audience to take action rather than postpone their decision indefinitely.

- **Limited-Time Offers**: Provide a discount or bonus resource for those who purchase by a specific deadline. For example, "Sign up by Friday to receive a free strategy workbook."
- **Enrollment Windows**: If your course includes live components or a cohort model, open enrollment only a few times per year. This exclusivity can drive demand.
- **Limited Spots**: If your course offers personalized feedback or one-on-one support, emphasize the limited availability.

However, it's essential to stay genuine—false urgency or scarcity erodes trust and damages your reputation.

Step 6: Engage Through Personalization

Modern consumers expect personalized experiences, and marketing your course should be no exception. Tailor your approach to make potential buyers feel seen and understood.

- **Segmented Email Campaigns**: Group your audience by their interests or stage in the buying process. Send targeted messages that address their specific concerns or questions.
- **Direct Messages**: Use Instagram DMs to connect personally with followers who show interest in your course. Answer their questions thoughtfully, without pressuring them to buy.

- **Interactive Content**: Polls, quizzes, and interactive stories on social media can help you learn more about your audience while subtly steering them toward your offer.

This level of attention deepens relationships and creates loyal fans who are more likely to convert.

Step 7: Leverage the Power of Community

A thriving community amplifies your marketing efforts and makes your audience feel part of something bigger. This connection drives both engagement and sales.

- Create a Facebook Group or private forum for your audience to share insights and ask questions. Use this space to demonstrate the value of your course.
- Offer exclusive perks to members who enroll in your course, such as live group coaching sessions or behind-the-scenes content.
- Encourage your students to share their progress and wins publicly, tagging you in their posts. These organic testimonials act as free advertising to their networks.

Step 8: Use Subtle Call-to-Actions (CTAs)

Finally, your marketing should always include a clear but subtle call to action. Instead of aggressive language like "Buy Now!", opt for inviting phrases such as:

- "Ready to transform your Instagram strategy? Learn more about my step-by-step course."
- "Download the free guide and take the first step toward your Instagram goals."
- "Enrollment closes soon—secure your spot today to start seeing results."

A well-crafted CTA guides your audience without making them feel pressured.

Selling Without Selling

The art of selling without feeling "salesy" lies in showing your audience that your course is not just a product but a solution they've been searching for. By serving instead of selling, telling stories that resonate, and building trust through value and authenticity, you create a magnetic presence that draws people to your offer. When executed with care, these strategies allow you to market confidently, knowing that your course is a gift worth sharing.

Chapter 5: Mastering Affiliate Marketing

Affiliate marketing, at its core, is about creating a symbiotic relationship between trust and value. It's a strategy that can transform content creators into income generators, but only when approached with authenticity and precision. The power of affiliate marketing lies in its simplicity: recommending products or services that resonate with your audience in exchange for a commission. Yet, the mastery of this art requires more than just placing links—it demands a deep understanding of your audience and an unwavering commitment to quality.

The journey to becoming an affiliate marketing expert begins with alignment. The products or services you endorse should seamlessly integrate with your brand identity. Imagine being an advocate for wellness and introducing your audience to a fitness app that has revolutionized your morning routines. Sharing a personal experience that underlines the benefits of the product transforms a mere recommendation into a powerful endorsement. Your audience isn't just buying a product; they're buying into your story, your expertise, and the trust you've cultivated over time.

To achieve this level of influence, you must dive into the art of storytelling. A recommendation without context is hollow, but a story rooted in personal experience or relatable scenarios is magnetic. Picture this: you're describing how a productivity tool helped you meet a critical deadline, balancing work and family life without breaking a sweat. This narrative not only highlights the product but also demonstrates its impact in a way that resonates deeply with your audience. It's not about selling; it's about showing.

However, trust doesn't come solely from authenticity. Transparency plays a pivotal role in affiliate marketing. Audiences today are perceptive and expect honesty. Disclosing your partnerships with a simple acknowledgment—"I may earn a small commission from this, but it won't cost you anything extra"—fosters trust and demonstrates your commitment to their best interests. Far from deterring potential buyers, transparency builds a relationship where your audience sees you as a partner in their decision-making process rather than a salesperson.

Execution is equally critical. It's one thing to recommend a product; it's another to make that recommendation easily actionable. Crafting engaging, valuable content around your affiliate links is essential. Whether it's a blog post, a podcast mention, or a YouTube tutorial, your content must provide enough insight to educate and entice. For instance, if you're showcasing a kitchen gadget, let your audience see it in action, highlighting its features while explaining how it simplifies your cooking process. When they click that link, they should feel confident that their purchase is backed by genuine utility and your stamp of approval.

The true mastery of affiliate marketing lies in the long game. This isn't a quick cash grab but a consistent effort to weave valuable recommendations into the fabric of your content. It's about understanding what your audience values most and meeting those needs with products that solve problems, save time, or elevate their lives. By staying authentic, creating compelling narratives, and maintaining transparency, affiliate marketing becomes more than just a revenue stream—it becomes an extension of your brand's mission to serve, inspire, and empower.

5.1 How Affiliate Marketing Works on Instagram

In the digital age, Instagram has evolved beyond being a platform for sharing snapshots of life—it has become a powerful engine for commerce. At the heart of this transformation lies affiliate marketing, a strategy that enables content creators to earn income by promoting products and services they believe in. But how does affiliate marketing thrive in the visually driven world of Instagram? It's a symphony of storytelling, strategy, and trust.

The first key to understanding affiliate marketing on Instagram is recognizing its unique environment. Unlike other platforms, Instagram operates on a visual-first principle. Here, your content isn't just seen; it's experienced. This makes Instagram the perfect playground for showcasing products in action, whether through high-quality images, immersive videos, or engaging Stories. For an affiliate marketer, this means creating content that doesn't just inform but captivates. When done right, your followers don't feel like they're being sold to; they feel like they're discovering something valuable through you.

Let's break down how it works. Affiliate marketing on Instagram typically revolves around affiliate links and unique discount codes. These tools track the sales or actions driven by your recommendations, ensuring that you receive credit for your efforts. While affiliate links are effective on blogs or websites, Instagram's structure presents a challenge: links aren't clickable in captions. This is where ingenuity comes in. You can place affiliate links in your bio, directing followers there with a call-to-action like, "Check the link in my bio for a special offer!" Alternatively, if you have over 10,000 followers or a verified account, the "Swipe Up" feature in Stories provides a seamless way to share links directly.

Success in Instagram affiliate marketing hinges on authenticity. Your audience follows you because they trust your voice and value your perspective. Promoting products that align with your niche and personal brand is non-negotiable. For instance, a fitness influencer might promote workout gear or health supplements, while a travel blogger might focus on luggage or booking services. Authenticity deepens when you showcase your genuine experience with the product—perhaps by sharing how a skincare product transformed your routine or how a gadget streamlined your daily tasks.

Engagement is another cornerstone. Instagram's algorithm favors content that sparks interaction, so your affiliate marketing efforts should focus on fostering conversations rather than simply broadcasting. Use captions to ask questions, such as, "What's your favorite way to stay organized?" alongside a post about a planner you're promoting. Polls, quizzes, and Q&A sessions in Stories can also create dynamic interactions while subtly spotlighting your affiliate products.

Finally, transparency is critical. Disclosing affiliate relationships builds trust with your audience and ensures compliance with advertising guidelines. A simple note like, "This post contains affiliate links, meaning I may earn a commission at no extra cost to you," not only adheres to regulations but also reinforces your honesty.

Affiliate marketing on Instagram is more than a revenue stream—it's an art. By blending creativity, authenticity, and strategic execution, you can transform your Instagram presence into a channel of influence, connection, and sustainable success.

5.2 Finding the Right Brands and Products to Promote

Affiliate marketing on Instagram thrives on authenticity, and nothing showcases your credibility more than aligning with the right brands and products. The process of choosing what to promote isn't just about profitability; it's about relevance, resonance, and responsibility. To build trust and sustain engagement, you must become a matchmaker, pairing your values and audience's needs with brands that reflect them.

The first step in identifying the right partnerships is understanding your niche and your audience. Who are your followers, and what are they looking for? A food blogger's audience might crave kitchen gadgets and gourmet spices, while a travel influencer's followers might be drawn to high-tech luggage or booking platforms. Knowing your audience's interests, challenges, and aspirations allows you to offer them products that solve their problems or enhance their lives.

Next, reflect on your brand. Authenticity is the foundation of influencer marketing, and promoting products that don't align with your ethos will erode trust. If you're a fitness coach advocating a healthy lifestyle, endorsing sugary drinks or fad diets could confuse your audience. Instead, focus on brands that complement your values, such as athletic wear, protein supplements, or wellness apps. This alignment ensures that every product you promote feels like a natural extension of your content.

When searching for potential partners, prioritize quality and reputation. Partnering with a brand that cuts corners or delivers subpar products can backfire, leaving your audience disappointed and skeptical of future recommendations. Do your homework—read reviews, test the product yourself, and, if possible, speak directly with the brand. Remember, you're not just promoting a product; you're endorsing an experience.

Once you've identified a promising brand, evaluate its affiliate program. Look for clear terms, competitive commission rates, and resources to support your success, such as promotional materials or access to an affiliate manager. Some programs offer tiered commissions, rewarding you more as your sales increase, while others might provide bonuses for new customer referrals. Platforms like ShareASale, Rakuten, and Amazon Associates host a variety of programs across industries, making them excellent starting points for discovery.

Your relationship with a brand should feel like a partnership, not a transaction. Establishing a connection with the company helps you create more authentic content. Reach out directly to brands you admire, even if they don't have a formal affiliate program. A well-crafted pitch explaining your audience, values, and vision can open doors to collaborations that feel meaningful.

Finally, keep an eye on trends while staying true to your identity. Seasonal products, emerging innovations, or viral sensations can generate buzz and engagement, but only if they fit your audience's interests. For instance, a fashion influencer might spotlight sustainable swimwear during summer or promote cozy knitwear in autumn.

Choosing the right brands and products isn't just about boosting revenue—it's about strengthening the relationship you have with your audience. When you consistently recommend items that genuinely add value, you not only enhance your credibility but also transform your

Instagram presence into a trusted resource. This blend of intentionality and authenticity is what sets successful affiliate marketers apart.

5.2 Creating Compelling Content That Converts

Understanding the Power of Storytelling

The most effective affiliate marketing content doesn't just inform—it captivates. At its core, compelling content leverages the art of storytelling to weave a narrative that resonates with your audience. Instead of simply describing a product's features, share an experience that highlights its benefits. If you're promoting a fitness tracker, recount a personal journey of improved health or productivity. By placing the product within a relatable context, you make it feel essential, not optional. People are more likely to trust recommendations that are wrapped in authenticity and anchored by emotion.

Addressing Your Audience's Pain Points

Conversions happen when content aligns with the needs of your audience. Begin by identifying their challenges and positioning the product as the solution. For example, if you're targeting new parents, a time-saving kitchen gadget could be framed as a lifesaver during sleepless nights. Show empathy for their struggles, then illustrate how the product eases those burdens. This approach creates a connection that makes your audience feel understood and valued. The stronger this emotional bond, the more likely they are to trust your endorsement and make a purchase.

Visual Content That Captures Attention

In the fast-paced world of Instagram, visual storytelling is non-negotiable. High-quality images, engaging videos, and dynamic reels are the cornerstones of effective affiliate marketing. Use vibrant and clear visuals that highlight the product's best features. For instance, an aesthetically pleasing flat lay of a skincare routine can draw in beauty enthusiasts, while a quick reel demonstrating a tech gadget's functionality can appeal to a more tech-savvy audience. Always ensure that your visuals are consistent with your personal brand's tone and style, reinforcing your authenticity.

Crafting Persuasive Captions

Your captions are where your voice shines. A compelling caption combines emotion, information, and a clear call to action (CTA). Start with a hook—a thought-provoking question, a surprising fact, or a relatable anecdote—to grab attention. Then, dive into how the product can enrich their lives. Keep your tone conversational and personal, as if you're recommending the product to a close friend. End with a strong CTA, like "Click the link in my bio to see why this has changed my daily routine." This clear direction encourages your audience to take the next step.

Leveraging Social Proof

Nothing builds trust like seeing others benefit from a product. Incorporate testimonials, reviews, or user-generated content to validate your claims. If the product has transformed your life, share before-and-after stories or results. This not only bolsters credibility but also alleviates skepticism. Highlight how the product is already making a difference in the lives of others, creating a sense of urgency and FOMO (fear of missing out).

Consistency in Content Delivery

Finally, consistency is key. One-off promotions rarely yield significant conversions. Instead, create a content calendar to integrate affiliate products seamlessly into your overall strategy. This repetition builds familiarity, reminding your audience of the product's value without feeling overly salesy. Whether it's a tutorial on Stories, a thoughtful post, or a reel showcasing the product in action, consistent exposure fosters trust and encourages long-term engagement.

By combining storytelling, empathy, and strategic delivery, you can craft affiliate marketing content that doesn't just sell but connects. When your audience feels seen, heard, and inspired, they'll naturally follow your lead.

5.4 Setting Up Automated Campaigns for Passive Revenue

The Promise of Automation

Imagine a system working tirelessly around the clock, promoting your affiliate links, nurturing potential buyers, and generating revenue—all while you focus on other aspects of your business or take a well-deserved break. This is the magic of automated campaigns. Automation transforms your marketing efforts into a streamlined machine, maximizing efficiency and minimizing the time required to manage promotions manually. It isn't just about saving effort; it's about creating a sustainable source of passive income that continues to grow with minimal intervention.

Choosing the Right Tools

The foundation of any successful automated campaign is the tools you choose. Email marketing platforms like Mailchimp, ConvertKit, or ActiveCampaign offer robust automation features tailored to affiliate marketers. These platforms allow you to design workflows that respond to your audience's behavior. For instance, if someone clicks on a link in your email but doesn't purchase, the system can send a follow-up email offering more details or a special incentive. Similarly, social media schedulers such as Buffer or Later ensure your affiliate content reaches your audience consistently, even when you're not actively posting.

Designing a High-Converting Funnel

An effective automated campaign begins with a well-designed funnel. Start by capturing leads through an engaging opt-in offer, such as a free guide, checklist, or webinar that aligns with the affiliate products you promote. Once you've collected their email addresses, nurture your leads with a sequence of emails designed to build trust and highlight the product's value. Each email should address a specific pain point or question your audience might have, progressively leading them closer to a purchase decision. This gradual approach ensures they feel informed and confident, not pressured.

Segmenting Your Audience

Automation shines brightest when you tailor your campaigns to the unique needs of your audience. Segmenting your subscribers based on their interests, behavior, or demographics ensures your messaging resonates deeply. For example, if you promote fitness equipment and skincare products, you can create separate workflows for those interested in each category. This precision not only increases the likelihood of conversions but also enhances the user experience, as subscribers receive content that feels personal and relevant.

Leveraging Retargeting Ads

Automation extends beyond emails. Retargeting ads on platforms like Facebook, Instagram, or Google Ads allow you to reach people who've interacted with your content but haven't taken the final step. By using tools like Facebook Pixel or Google Analytics, you can create automated ads that remind potential customers of the benefits of your affiliate product. This consistent presence keeps your offerings top-of-mind and increases the chances of conversion.

Monitoring and Optimizing Campaigns

Even the best-automated campaigns require periodic evaluation. Use analytics to monitor key metrics such as click-through rates, conversion rates, and revenue generated. Identify which parts of your workflow perform well and which need adjustment. Automation tools often provide insights into user behavior, enabling you to refine your approach for maximum impact. With regular optimization, your campaigns evolve alongside your audience, staying relevant and effective.

The Reward of Passive Revenue

When set up correctly, automated campaigns unlock the dream of earning passive income. They transform the hard work of creating and promoting content into a consistent revenue stream, allowing you to scale your affiliate marketing efforts without being tethered to constant management. This strategic investment of time and resources not only pays off in financial returns but also grants you the freedom to focus on the bigger picture of your business and life goals.

Chapter 6: Automating Your Income Streams

The Power of Automation in Building Wealth

In the ever-evolving world of digital entrepreneurship, the most successful individuals don't simply work harder—they work smarter. One of the most profound shifts in business today is the ability to automate income streams, allowing your business to generate revenue passively. The key to financial freedom isn't necessarily about doing more, but about creating systems that work on your behalf, even when you're not actively involved. Automating income streams allows you to step back from the daily grind and watch your wealth grow.

Setting Up Passive Income Foundations

The first step in automating your income is laying the groundwork for passive revenue streams. These are the engines that will keep generating money with minimal effort on your part once set in motion. Think of passive income as the fuel for your business that doesn't require constant attention. Examples of passive income include selling digital products like eBooks or online courses, running membership sites, and affiliate marketing. Each of these income sources works tirelessly for you while you sleep, as long as the systems that support them are in place.

Leveraging Technology for Streamlined Operations

The backbone of income automation is technology. Platforms like Shopify for eCommerce, Teachable or Thinkific for online courses, and Patreon for memberships, allow creators to set up and sell products or services with minimal involvement. Once these systems are in place, they handle payment processing, order fulfillment, and customer service, leaving you to focus on scaling your business and reaching new customers. These tools have revolutionized the way entrepreneurs run their operations, enabling them to serve hundreds or thousands of clients simultaneously without being bogged down by daily tasks.

Automating Affiliate Marketing

Affiliate marketing is one of the most straightforward ways to generate automated income. Once you've selected the right products to promote and created engaging content, the rest of the process can be automated. Email marketing platforms, such as ConvertKit or ActiveCampaign, can send personalized messages to your audience, encouraging them to purchase through your affiliate links. Similarly, tools like Buffer or Hootsuite can schedule social media posts that include affiliate links, ensuring that your promotion continues even when you're not online. By automating the content distribution process, affiliate marketing can become a consistent revenue stream without constant manual effort.

Creating a Sales Funnel That Works for You

A well-designed sales funnel is the cornerstone of automated income. It's the customer journey that begins when a prospect first encounters your content and ends when they make a purchase. The beauty of automation lies in the funnel's ability to nurture leads through email sequences, upsells, and retargeting ads without any further intervention from you. A carefully constructed funnel builds trust with potential customers, offering value at every stage, and guiding them towards purchasing your product or service. Tools like ClickFunnels or Kartra simplify the process of building such automated funnels, enabling you to focus on creating high-quality content that attracts your ideal audience.

Managing and Scaling Your Systems

While automation allows you to create a passive income stream, it doesn't mean you can set it and forget it completely. Monitoring and optimization are still essential to success. Analytics tools integrated with most platforms give you detailed insights into how your income streams are performing, helping you identify what's working and what needs improvement. For example, if your email campaigns aren't converting as well as you'd like, automation platforms allow you to adjust your content or segment your audience for better results. By regularly analyzing and tweaking your systems, you ensure that your passive income grows and becomes more efficient over time.

The Rewards of Automation

Automating your income streams offers unparalleled freedom. It allows you to focus on other areas of your business—such as innovation, content creation, or scaling—while your automated systems work behind the scenes. The more systems you implement, the more your business can function without constant oversight. For many entrepreneurs, this isn't just about making money; it's about designing a lifestyle where work isn't the central focus. Automation gives you the ability to live life on your terms, freeing up time for the things that matter most, all while your business continues to thrive.

The beauty of automating your income streams is that it creates a future where your efforts today pay dividends tomorrow. By embracing automation, you aren't just working for money—you're building systems that ensure your financial growth is both sustainable and scalable. In the world of entrepreneurship, this is the key to long-term success and the ultimate reward.

6.1 Tools for Streamlining Content Creation and Scheduling

The Need for Efficient Content Creation

In the fast-paced world of digital marketing, content is king. However, creating high-quality content consistently can quickly become overwhelming, especially when you are managing multiple platforms. To stand out and remain relevant, content creators must consistently produce material that is not only engaging but also timely. This is where tools for streamlining content creation and scheduling come into play. These tools are designed to simplify and automate the more tedious aspects of content creation, allowing you to focus on what truly matters: your creativity and engagement with your audience.

Harnessing the Power of Content Creation Tools

The first step in streamlining your content creation process is choosing the right tools that match your needs. Tools like Canva and Adobe Spark have revolutionized content creation, making it easier for even non-designers to craft professional-looking visuals. These platforms come with pre-built templates, design assets, and intuitive drag-and-drop features, which allow you to create stunning graphics in a fraction of the time it once took. With these tools, you no longer need to spend hours designing from scratch or waiting for a graphic designer to deliver. Instead, you can create posts, infographics, and even marketing materials on your own, giving you more control over your content and saving time.

Another indispensable tool for content creation is Grammarly, which ensures that your written content is free of errors. Whether you're writing social media posts, blog articles, or email newsletters, Grammarly's real-time editing feature helps you maintain a polished and professional tone. It's a must-have for anyone looking to create error-free, impactful copy that resonates with their audience.

Scheduling Tools for Seamless Content Delivery

Once you have your content ready, scheduling it efficiently is the next challenge. Without proper scheduling, it's easy to fall behind on posting or forget important deadlines. This is where tools like Buffer, Hootsuite, and Later come in. These platforms allow you to plan and schedule your posts across multiple social media channels in advance. By doing so, you can ensure that your content goes live at optimal times, even when you're away from your desk.

The beauty of these scheduling tools lies in their ability to automate the posting process while still providing you with flexibility. You can set a posting schedule, monitor engagement in real-time, and adjust your strategy based on performance metrics—all without manually posting each time. These platforms allow you to tailor your posting times to your audience's behavior, maximizing the likelihood of engagement and interaction.

Collaborative Tools for Streamlining Workflow

In a collaborative environment, efficiency is crucial. Whether you're working with a team or outsourcing specific tasks, tools like Trello and Asana can help keep your content creation process organized. These project management platforms allow you to track deadlines, assign tasks, and streamline communication between team members. With Trello, for example, you can create boards for each project, break down tasks into actionable steps, and keep everyone on the same page.

Asana offers similar features but with additional capabilities for tracking project timelines and integrating with other tools like Google Drive or Slack. By centralizing your workflow, these tools ensure that content creation runs smoothly, and no deadlines are missed.

Optimizing Content Strategy with Analytics

Once you've started creating and scheduling content, the next step is to track its performance. Tools like Google Analytics, Instagram Insights, and Facebook Analytics provide valuable data on how your content is performing across different platforms. By analyzing metrics such as engagement, clicks, and shares, you can refine your content strategy to better meet the needs and interests of your audience. These insights not only help you adjust your content but also enable you to make data-driven decisions for future posts, ensuring that your content continues to resonate with your target audience.

The right tools for streamlining content creation and scheduling can transform the way you approach your digital marketing efforts. By using platforms that enhance your creativity, automate your scheduling, and track your performance, you can ensure that your content creation process is not only more efficient but also more effective. As a result, you'll be able to maintain a consistent presence across multiple channels, engage with your audience meaningfully, and grow your digital presence—all while freeing up valuable time to focus on other aspects of your business.

The key is finding the right combination of tools that work for you and continuously refining your approach as your needs evolve.

6.2 Email Marketing Funnels and Instagram Integration

The Power of Email Marketing

In the ever-evolving world of digital marketing, email remains one of the most powerful tools at your disposal. Despite the rise of social media and other communication platforms, email marketing continues to deliver the highest return on investment (ROI) for businesses of all sizes. The reason for this is simple: email allows for personalized communication that speaks directly to the individual, fostering a stronger connection with your audience. However, creating a successful email marketing strategy goes beyond just sending out a newsletter. To truly harness its potential, you must build an email marketing funnel—an automated system that nurtures your leads, converts them into customers, and keeps them engaged over time.

Understanding Email Marketing Funnels

An email marketing funnel is a series of emails designed to guide potential customers through a process, from initial awareness to conversion, and ultimately, loyalty. The funnel typically consists of three stages: awareness, engagement, and conversion. In the awareness phase, your goal is to capture the attention of your target audience and get them to opt into your email list. This is often done through lead magnets such as free resources, discounts, or exclusive content that entice people to subscribe.

Once they're on your list, the engagement phase begins. Here, you provide valuable content that nurtures the relationship you've started. This could include helpful tips, behind-the-scenes content, or special offers that speak to their interests and pain points. The final stage is conversion, where your email content shifts toward promoting your product or service in a way that feels natural and aligned with the value you've already provided. This phase often includes calls-to-action (CTAs), testimonials, or limited-time offers that encourage recipients to take the next step.

Integrating Instagram with Your Funnel

Instagram, with its visual appeal and highly engaged user base, is the perfect platform to complement your email marketing efforts. While email marketing allows for in-depth, long-form communication, Instagram gives you a chance to reach your audience more spontaneously and visually. By integrating Instagram into your email marketing funnel, you can create a seamless experience for your audience that builds trust and encourages conversion.

One of the most effective ways to integrate Instagram with your email funnel is by using Instagram as a tool for lead generation. Use Instagram Stories, posts, and even Reels to offer exclusive content or lead magnets that encourage followers to subscribe to your email list. For instance, you might share a snippet of a valuable resource in your Story and then provide a link that directs followers to a landing page where they can opt-in to receive the full resource. This approach creates a direct connection between your Instagram audience and your email funnel, allowing you to expand your reach and nurture new leads more effectively.

Another strategy is using Instagram to promote your email content. If you have a new email campaign going out, tease it on your Instagram account to build anticipation. You could share a behind-the-scenes look at what's inside your next email or even provide a preview of a special offer that will be sent to your subscribers. This kind of cross-promotion not only boosts engagement on both platforms but also encourages your Instagram followers to join your email list to access the full content.

Building a Cohesive Experience Across Platforms

When integrating Instagram and email marketing funnels, consistency is key. Ensure that the messaging and visual branding across both platforms align. For example, if you're using Instagram to promote a limited-time offer, your email should follow suit, reinforcing the same offer in a way that feels cohesive. This consistency creates a seamless journey for your audience, whether they're engaging with your content on Instagram or reading your latest email.

Additionally, make use of Instagram's built-in features like swipe-up links or the "Link in Bio" option to drive traffic to your email sign-up page. By simplifying the process and making it easy for users to take action, you increase the likelihood that your followers will convert into email subscribers.

The Long-Term Benefits of Integration

Integrating Instagram with your email marketing funnel is not just about short-term sales—it's about building a long-term relationship with your audience. By using Instagram to drive leads into your funnel and then nurturing them through personalized, valuable email content, you create a community of engaged, loyal followers who are more likely to become repeat customers. This kind of relationship-building is essential for sustainable business growth, as it moves beyond transactional interactions to create a deeper connection with your audience.

In the end, combining the visual appeal of Instagram with the power of email marketing funnels allows you to build a more robust and effective marketing strategy. When done correctly, this integration can drive conversions, increase engagement, and help you cultivate an audience that not only buys from you but actively supports your brand over the long term. The key is to create an experience that feels natural, personalized, and seamless, allowing each platform to complement and enhance the other.

6.3 Passive Income Blueprint: Setting Up Systems That Run Themselves

The Promise of Passive Income

One of the most alluring promises in the world of entrepreneurship is the concept of passive income. Imagine a scenario where, while you're sleeping, traveling, or enjoying time with family, money is still flowing into your bank account. It's the dream many aspire to, yet the reality of setting up such a system often feels elusive. But with the right strategies, tools, and mindset, creating a passive income stream that runs itself isn't just a fantasy—it's an achievable goal. The key to unlocking passive income is in setting up systems that require minimal ongoing effort to maintain, allowing your business to grow and generate revenue without constant attention.

Automating Your Offerings

The first step in creating a truly passive income stream is to automate the products or services you're offering. Digital products, such as eBooks, online courses, or membership sites, are ideal candidates for this type of automation. Once created, they require very little effort to sell and deliver. With the right sales funnels in place, these products can be marketed automatically, with systems in place to handle everything from processing payments to delivering the products to your customers.

For example, an online course can be set up to be sold through an automated funnel. You can run Facebook ads or use Instagram to drive traffic to a landing page where visitors can learn more about the course and sign up. Once they've enrolled, the course content is delivered automatically through a learning management system (LMS), while automated emails nurture the students and encourage them to continue their journey. By building this type of infrastructure, you've created a product that essentially sells itself, leaving you free to focus on other projects or expand your offerings.

Streamlining Customer Communication

Another pillar of passive income is effective communication. While it may seem counterintuitive, one of the best ways to ensure that communication remains personal without requiring a constant time commitment is through automation. Email marketing sequences, for example, can be set up to send tailored messages to potential or existing customers at specific intervals. These emails can welcome new subscribers, offer them discounts, or provide them with valuable content that nurtures the relationship over time.

By using tools like ConvertKit, Mailchimp, or ActiveCampaign, you can set up complex email funnels that automatically send personalized messages based on user behavior. When a customer purchases one of your products, for instance, they could be automatically sent a thank-you email, followed by a series of emails that upsell related products or encourage them to leave a review. These automated communications keep customers engaged and nurtured, driving additional revenue without requiring any additional effort from you.

Building a Self-Sustaining Marketing System

Once your products and communication systems are automated, the next step is to create a marketing engine that works on autopilot. The beauty of modern digital marketing lies in the ability to leverage organic and paid strategies that run 24/7. Search engine optimization (SEO) ensures that your content ranks highly in search results, driving organic traffic to your website and funnel pages. Paid advertising, such as Facebook or Instagram ads, can be set up to target specific audiences and run continuously, adjusting based on performance.

Another powerful tool in building a passive income system is affiliate marketing. By setting up an affiliate program for your digital products, you can recruit others to promote and sell for you. In exchange, affiliates earn a commission for each sale they generate. This allows you to scale your business exponentially without having to increase your workload. As affiliates continue to promote your products, your passive income grows, all without any extra effort from your side.

Outsourcing to Free Up Your Time

While automation can take care of much of the work, there are still tasks that might require a human touch. For these tasks, outsourcing is the key to freeing up your time and ensuring your business continues to run smoothly. Virtual assistants, freelance content creators, or marketing specialists can handle everything from managing your email lists to producing new content or even dealing with customer service inquiries. By leveraging the skills of others, you create a support system that allows you to continue growing your passive income without getting bogged down in day-to-day operations.

Consistency and Long-Term Vision

Building a passive income stream isn't a "get rich quick" solution. It requires time, effort, and strategic planning to create systems that will eventually run on their own. But once these systems are in place, the work required to maintain them is minimal compared to the rewards they generate. Passive income is about consistency—consistently delivering value to your customers, improving your systems, and optimizing your marketing efforts. With patience and dedication, you can create a business that generates income with minimal intervention.

The Freedom to Live Your Life

Ultimately, the true benefit of passive income is the freedom it provides. When you've set up systems that run themselves, you're no longer tied to your business in the traditional sense. You can choose to work on new projects, take vacations, or even step away from your business for a while, knowing that your income is still flowing. This freedom allows you to live life on your terms, with the peace of mind that comes from having a sustainable, self-sufficient business.

In conclusion, setting up passive income streams requires a combination of strategic planning, automation, and smart delegation. By automating your offerings, streamlining communication, and building self-sustaining marketing systems, you can create a business that generates income on autopilot. The result is a life of freedom and flexibility, where the systems you've put in place allow you to enjoy the fruits of your labor while continuing to grow your wealth.

6.4 Time Management Hacks for Scaling

The Challenge of Scaling

As your business grows, so do the demands on your time. What once seemed manageable—responding to emails, creating content, fulfilling customer orders—suddenly becomes a full-fledged operation. Scaling a business often feels like juggling too many balls in the air. You want to grow, but you're faced with the growing pains of increased responsibilities and tasks. The truth is, that without effective time management, scaling can become overwhelming. But with the right strategies in place, you can streamline your processes and manage your time wisely, creating a business that thrives without sacrificing your personal life.

Prioritizing Your Most Important Tasks

One of the first steps to managing your time effectively is learning to prioritize. Not every task is of equal importance, and when you're scaling, you need to focus on what truly moves the needle. The first task is identifying the activities that directly contribute to your business's growth, such as developing new products, creating high-quality content, or optimizing your marketing efforts. Once you've pinpointed these critical areas, focus the majority of your time on them.

It's easy to get sidetracked by less important activities—sorting through emails, reorganizing your workspace, or handling small administrative tasks. While these may be necessary, they don't directly contribute to your growth. By categorizing tasks based on their impact and urgency, you can make better decisions about where to focus your energy.

Time Blocking for Focused Work

Time blocking is an incredibly effective technique for managing your schedule. The principle behind time blocking is simple: you dedicate specific chunks of time to focused work on certain tasks. Instead of trying to multitask or allowing distractions to pull you away from your goals, you set clear, uninterrupted periods for deep work.

For instance, you might set aside two hours every morning to focus exclusively on product development or content creation. During this time, you avoid checking emails, social media, or taking calls. By setting clear boundaries around your time, you're ensuring that you stay focused and productive, which allows you to make faster progress as you scale your business.

Delegating to the Right People

Scaling doesn't mean doing everything yourself—it's about building a team that supports your vision and frees up your time for the tasks that truly matter. Delegation is a key time management hack that allows you to focus on your strengths while empowering others to handle the work you may not have the time or expertise for.

Consider which aspects of your business you can delegate. Perhaps you need a virtual assistant to manage customer inquiries or a social media manager to handle your Instagram posts. By trusting others to take on these responsibilities, you can concentrate on high-level decision-making and strategic planning. Investing in a skilled team may feel like an additional expense at first, but it's an investment in your ability to scale faster and more efficiently.

Automating Repetitive Tasks

When scaling your business, automation is your best friend. Many tasks that once required manual input—like email marketing, scheduling social media posts, and processing orders—can now be automated through tools and software. Automation not only saves time but also reduces the chance of human error and allows you to focus on the bigger picture.

For example, using a tool like Buffer or Hootsuite to schedule your social media posts frees up hours each week that would otherwise be spent manually posting content. Similarly, email automation tools like

ConvertKit or Mailchimp allow you to set up email sequences that engage and nurture your audience without having to write every email individually. Automating these processes enables you to keep your business running smoothly while freeing up more time to focus on growth.

Learning to Say No

As your business expands, you'll face an increasing number of opportunities, requests, and distractions. While it's tempting to say yes to everything, this can quickly lead to burnout and overwhelm. Part of effective time management is learning to say no to things that don't align with your priorities or long-term goals.

When scaling, it's crucial to stay focused on what matters most. If a new opportunity or collaboration doesn't fit within your strategic plan or if it pulls you away from your key growth activities, it's okay to turn it down. Saying no isn't about being unkind—it's about protecting your time and energy for the things that truly support your growth.

Taking Time to Rest and Recharge

Finally, it's important to remember that time management isn't just about working harder or longer hours. To scale your business effectively, you need to be at your best—physically, mentally, and emotionally. This means taking time to rest, recharge, and maintain a healthy work-life balance.

When you're well-rested and energized, your decision-making is sharper, your creativity flows more freely, and your ability to focus is enhanced. Don't neglect self-care in the pursuit of growth. Make sure to schedule time for breaks, exercise, and personal activities that help you maintain a healthy balance. After all, a successful business needs a healthy entrepreneur at its helm.

Scaling your business requires discipline, strategy, and the ability to manage your time effectively. By prioritizing high-impact tasks, using time blocking, delegating work, automating repetitive tasks, and setting boundaries, you can create the space you need to grow without feeling overwhelmed. Time management isn't about working harder—it's about working smarter, and by adopting the right time management hacks, you can build a thriving business while preserving your well-being.

Chapter 7: Scaling Beyond Instagram

The Evolution of Your Digital Presence

Instagram is an incredible platform, but its magic lies in its ability to act as a launchpad for bigger opportunities. While it provides a powerful foundation for building brand recognition, fostering community, and driving sales, long-term growth requires diversifying your digital presence. Relying solely on one platform puts your business at risk. Algorithm changes, platform outages, or shifts in user behavior can disrupt even the most well-thought-out strategies. Scaling beyond Instagram allows you to secure your business and expand your reach in ways that amplify your impact.

Creating a Multi-Channel Strategy

Scaling beyond Instagram begins with a multi-channel approach. The goal is not to abandon what works but to enhance it by establishing a presence on complementary platforms. Consider which platforms align best with your audience and your business goals. For instance, TikTok offers short, viral content to younger audiences, while LinkedIn is ideal for B2B relationships and thought leadership.

Each channel brings unique opportunities to repurpose and expand your content. A tutorial posted on Instagram can become a full-length video on YouTube, a blog post on your website, and a snippet for Pinterest. By tailoring content to each platform while maintaining a consistent brand voice, you ensure your message resonates across diverse audiences.

Building an Owned Audience with Email Marketing

While social platforms are powerful, they don't give you ownership of your audience. This is where email marketing becomes indispensable. By encouraging your Instagram followers to join your email list, you establish a direct line of communication that isn't subject to algorithms or platform rules.

Offer valuable incentives, such as free resources, exclusive discounts, or behind-the-scenes content, to encourage sign-ups. Once you have your email list, create engaging campaigns that nurture relationships and drive sales. Newsletters, personalized recommendations, and updates keep your audience connected and invested in your brand.

Developing a Website as Your Digital Hub

A professional website serves as the cornerstone of your online presence beyond Instagram. It's a space you own entirely, free from the limitations of social platforms. Your website should reflect your brand identity while functioning as a hub for all your content, products, and services.

Consider incorporating features like a blog to share in-depth insights, an online store to sell your products, and an FAQ section to address common customer questions. Your website also enhances credibility and provides a central location where followers from multiple platforms can learn more about you.

Exploring Paid Advertising and Partnerships

Expanding your reach often involves strategic investments in paid advertising. Platforms like Google Ads, Facebook, and YouTube offer opportunities to target audiences beyond your Instagram followers. By experimenting with different ad formats and targeting methods, you can drive traffic to your website, increase email sign-ups, and generate leads from new demographics.

Additionally, partnerships with influencers, brands, or affiliates on other platforms introduce you to fresh audiences. Collaborations provide social proof and amplify your brand's voice, creating win-win opportunities for mutual growth.

Scaling with Systems and Analytics

As you expand your digital footprint, systems and analytics become essential for sustainable growth. Use tools to schedule and automate content across platforms, ensuring consistency while freeing up time. Regularly review performance metrics to understand which strategies are delivering results.

Analyze engagement rates, conversion metrics, and audience behaviors to refine your approach. Scaling is not about doing everything at once—it's about doing the right things, tracking progress, and iterating for success.

Scaling beyond Instagram isn't about replacing the platform but building a robust ecosystem where your brand thrives across multiple channels. By diversifying your presence, creating owned assets like email lists and websites, and leveraging partnerships and analytics, you safeguard your business against unpredictability while reaching new heights. Instagram may be the spark, but true growth lies in the fire you build beyond it.

7.1 Diversifying Income Streams Across Platforms

The Importance of Diversification

Relying on a single platform or revenue stream is akin to building a house on one pillar—it might stand for a while, but the risk of collapse is ever-present. Diversifying income streams across platforms is not just a smart business strategy; it's a necessity for sustainable growth. Platforms evolve, trends shift, and audiences migrate. A diversified approach ensures that your brand remains adaptable and resilient in the face of change.

This journey begins by understanding where your audience spends their time and identifying complementary opportunities for monetization. By strategically expanding your presence, you can tap into new revenue streams without diluting your core brand identity.

Repurposing Content for New Opportunities

One of the simplest ways to diversify income streams is through repurposing content. A single piece of content, like an Instagram tutorial or an insightful post, can become the foundation for multiple streams of income when adapted for different platforms.

For example, a detailed Instagram caption on productivity hacks could be expanded into a full blog post for your website, a YouTube video tutorial, or even a downloadable guide available for purchase. Platforms like TikTok or Pinterest could further amplify this content, each attracting different segments of your audience.

The key is to tailor your content to each platform's unique strengths while maintaining consistency in tone and branding. By doing so, you extend the lifespan and reach of your ideas, increasing the likelihood of turning views into sales.

Monetizing Beyond Social Media

Social media is an excellent starting point for building an audience, but long-term success involves moving beyond it. Email marketing offers a reliable channel for nurturing deeper relationships with your followers. Create exclusive content, courses, or membership communities to monetize directly. Platforms like Patreon, Substack, or even your website can host paid content that your audience is willing to invest in because of the value you provide.

E-commerce is another powerful avenue. If your audience resonates with your brand's aesthetics or mission, consider launching a merchandise line or branded products. Whether it's digital downloads, physical goods, or collaborations with other brands, a well-curated store can quickly become a substantial income source.

Leveraging Affiliate Marketing and Sponsored Partnerships

Affiliate marketing and sponsored partnerships are natural extensions of a diversified strategy. Through affiliate marketing, you can recommend products or services that align with your audience's interests while earning a commission. The trust you've built ensures that recommendations feel genuine, increasing conversion rates.

Similarly, brand sponsorships allow you to collaborate with companies that share your values. However, authenticity is crucial. Carefully vetting partnerships ensures that your audience continues to see you as a trusted authority rather than a sales-driven influencer.

Building Longevity Through Passive Revenue

Passive income streams, such as digital products, online courses, or evergreen content, are the gold standard for diversification. These assets require an upfront effort but continue generating revenue with minimal ongoing work. A well-designed digital course or an evergreen blog post optimized for search engines can bring in consistent earnings while you focus on other aspects of your business.

Integrating passive revenue into your strategy not only stabilizes income but also frees up time to explore new opportunities, innovate, and scale your brand.

The Synergy of Multiple Streams

When done correctly, diversification creates synergy among platforms and revenue streams. A blog post drives traffic to your e-commerce store; an Instagram post builds email subscribers; a YouTube video promotes an affiliate link. Each channel feeds the others, creating a dynamic ecosystem where growth becomes exponential.

By focusing on diversification, you future-proof your business while maximizing your impact and income. It's not about being everywhere at once but about being intentional and strategic in your expansion. With a clear vision and a diversified approach, you can turn your brand into a multi-platform powerhouse.

7.2 Repurposing Content for Maximum Impact

The Art of Multiplication

Creating content is an investment of time, energy, and creativity. Repurposing that content is the art of multiplying its value, turning a single idea into a wealth of opportunities across platforms. It's a strategy rooted in efficiency and designed to amplify your reach. At its core, repurposing allows you to extend the life of your content, ensuring that each piece resonates with as many people as possible while fitting seamlessly into different formats and audiences.

The secret to successful repurposing lies in identifying the essence of your message. Whether it's an Instagram post, a blog article, or a video, your goal is to extract the most powerful elements and adapt them to fit other mediums without losing their impact.

Tailoring for the Platform

Each platform has its unique language and audience preferences. Instagram thrives on visual storytelling, while YouTube values in-depth exploration, and Twitter rewards brevity. Repurposing isn't a matter of copying and pasting; it's about reimagining the message to suit the environment.

Consider an educational Instagram carousel post. The same concept could become a detailed blog article for your website, offering additional insights and resources. That blog could then be distilled into a 60-second TikTok tip or expanded into a live Q&A session on Facebook. By tailoring your content, you ensure it feels native to the platform while preserving its original purpose.

Reaching New Audiences

Not every member of your audience consumes content in the same way. Some prefer to scroll through quick updates on social media, while others enjoy longer reads or engaging videos. By repurposing your content, you cater to different preferences, broadening your audience and deepening their connection to your brand.

For instance, a podcast episode packed with value might inspire a series of Instagram quotes, a blog post summarizing the key takeaways, and an email newsletter with a call to action. Each format allows you to connect with a distinct audience segment while reinforcing the same overarching message.

Optimizing for Longevity

Another advantage of repurposing is the ability to breathe new life into older content. Evergreen topics—those that remain relevant over time—are particularly well-suited for this strategy. A popular Instagram post from a year ago can be updated with fresh insights and transformed into a new blog post or video. This approach not only saves time but also ensures that your content library continues to work for you long after its initial release.

Repurposing also helps with search engine optimization. A single blog post adapted into various formats creates multiple touchpoints for your audience to discover your brand. These interconnected pieces of content enhance your visibility, leading to a compounding effect on traffic and engagement.

Maximizing Impact Through Consistency

The key to repurposing effectively is maintaining consistency in your brand voice and messaging. While the format and delivery may change, the underlying tone and purpose should remain cohesive. This consistency helps build trust with your audience, ensuring they recognize your content regardless of where they encounter it.

Repurposing isn't just a time-saving tactic; it's a way to amplify your influence, ensuring that your ideas resonate across platforms and reach their full potential. By mastering this skill, you transform each piece of content into a building block for a more expansive and impactful presence.

7.3 Collaborations, Sponsorships, and Partnerships

The Power of Strategic Alliances

In the dynamic landscape of digital entrepreneurship, collaborations, sponsorships, and partnerships represent a powerful trifecta for growth.

These alliances transcend mere monetary benefits; they amplify your brand's reach, infuse fresh perspectives, and establish credibility in competitive markets. By aligning with the right collaborators, you can unlock opportunities that would take years to achieve alone.

At its core, a strategic partnership is about mutual benefit. The key lies in finding brands, influencers, or creators whose values and audience align with yours. Authenticity is critical; collaborations that feel forced or disconnected risk alienating your audience rather than engaging them.

Collaborations: Amplifying Influence

Collaborations between creators or businesses can generate buzz and open doors to new audiences. Whether it's a co-branded product, a joint live event, or a shared social media campaign, collaborations are a way to pool resources and expand your influence.

Consider a fitness influencer teaming up with a nutritionist to create a holistic wellness guide. The fitness expert's audience gains insight into healthy eating, while the nutritionist's followers learn the importance of exercise. Both parties win by offering added value to their respective audiences while enhancing their credibility in their shared niche.

Collaboration success hinges on shared goals and effective communication. When both parties invest equal effort and share a unified vision, the synergy can produce results far greater than individual efforts.

Sponsorships: Monetizing Connections

Sponsorships provide a direct path to monetization. When brands sponsor your content, they're not just buying exposure; they're investing in the trust you've built with your audience. For this reason, choosing sponsors should be approached with care.

A sponsorship that aligns with your brand's ethos can feel like a natural extension of your message. For instance, a travel blogger endorsing a sustainable luggage brand strengthens their advocacy for eco-conscious travel while offering their audience a product they may genuinely appreciate. Conversely, mismatched sponsorships can erode trust and harm your reputation.

Successful sponsorships are built on transparency. Disclosing paid partnerships not only complies with ethical guidelines but also strengthens your audience's trust. Audiences today value honesty and are more likely to support influencers who are upfront about their collaborations.

Partnerships: Long-Term Impact

While collaborations and sponsorships often have shorter time frames, partnerships are about building long-term relationships. These alliances might involve co-creating content over months, developing exclusive products, or launching campaigns that evolve.

An example of a successful partnership could be a tech influencer working with a software company to co-develop a product that solves a specific user problem. Such partnerships allow you to tap into the partner's resources and expertise while sharing the workload and risks.

Partnerships thrive on trust and shared commitment. Regular communication, clearly defined roles, and mutual respect form the backbone of any enduring alliance.

Unlocking Growth Through Connection

Collaborations, sponsorships, and partnerships are not merely transactional; they are transformative. By embracing these opportunities, you expand your brand's horizons and create a richer experience for your audience. The secret to thriving in these relationships lies in authenticity, alignment, and a commitment to adding value. With the right approach, strategic alliances can catapult your brand into new realms of success.

7.4 Staying Ahead of Social Media Trends

The Ever-Changing Landscape of Social Media

Social media evolves at a relentless pace, driven by new technologies, user behaviors, and platform innovations. What works today may be outdated tomorrow. Staying ahead of these trends isn't just a matter of relevance—it's about positioning yourself as a thought leader who adapts and thrives in a shifting digital ecosystem. Those who anticipate changes and embrace them early not only maintain their influence but also set themselves apart as innovators.

The first step in staying ahead is understanding that trends often emerge from user behaviors, not platforms themselves. By observing how audiences interact with content, you can identify patterns before they become mainstream. This proactive approach allows you to pivot strategies and test new ideas ahead of your competition.

Listening to the Platforms

Each social media platform has a rhythm of its own, marked by algorithm updates and feature launches. Paying close attention to these changes can be a goldmine for growth opportunities. Platforms like Instagram, TikTok, and LinkedIn often reward early adopters of new features. For instance, when Instagram introduced Reels, creators who jumped on the format immediately experienced increased reach as the platform prioritized this content in user feeds.

Keeping an ear to the ground means more than following official announcements; it involves observing how these updates are being adopted by creators and businesses. Participate in beta tests if available, and experiment with new features to understand their potential. By doing so, you not only learn the mechanics but also stand out as a leader willing to innovate.

The Role of Analytics in Trendspotting

Data is your most reliable guide in navigating social media trends. Analytics tools, whether native to the platform or third-party services provide insights into which types of content resonate with your audience. Analyzing engagement patterns can reveal shifts in preferences, such as a growing interest in short-form video or interactive polls.

Use this data to experiment with formats that align with emerging trends. While it's essential to follow data-driven strategies, leave room for creativity and spontaneity. Sometimes, the most viral content emerges from a bold, untested idea that taps into the zeitgeist.

Building a Trend-Resilient Brand

While adapting to trends is critical, your brand's core identity should remain stable. Jumping on every fad can dilute your message and confuse your audience. Instead, filter trends through the lens of your brand values. Ask yourself: Does this align with my mission? Will this serve my audience's needs? By grounding your decisions in your brand's purpose, you ensure that your trend-driven strategies remain authentic and impactful.

Looking Beyond the Horizon

To stay ahead, you must look where others aren't. Emerging platforms, cultural movements, and advancements in technology often offer clues about the future of social media. Virtual reality, augmented reality, and AI-driven content personalization are no longer just buzzwords—they are shaping the next wave of digital interaction.

Engaging with thought leaders, participating in industry events, and staying curious about innovations outside your immediate niche can provide the foresight needed to adapt and lead. Staying ahead of social media trends isn't about chasing every new idea—it's about discerning which ones align with your vision and audience, and then executing them with authenticity and finesse.

Chapter 8: Overcoming Challenges and Sustaining Growth

Embracing the Inevitable Challenges

Success in any endeavor, especially in the dynamic world of digital entrepreneurship, comes with its share of obstacles. These challenges often feel like unscalable walls, yet they are stepping stones in disguise.

Whether it's algorithm changes that decimate your reach or the mental fatigue of consistently creating content, every difficulty presents an opportunity to learn and grow.

One of the most common hurdles is maintaining momentum after an initial burst of success. The excitement of new projects often wanes as the grind of execution sets in. This is where resilience becomes your greatest asset. By anticipating setbacks as part of the journey rather than exceptions, you can reframe your perspective and approach challenges with a problem-solving mindset.

The Power of Adaptability

In the fast-paced digital landscape, rigidity is the enemy of progress. Adaptability allows you to navigate shifting market demands, audience behaviors, and technological advancements. For instance, when video content began dominating social media platforms, many creators who were rooted in static posts struggled to retain engagement. Those who adapted by embracing video storytelling not only survived the shift but thrived in it.

Adapting doesn't mean abandoning your core principles. Instead, it involves finding new ways to express your brand's identity. Conduct regular audits of your strategies and be open to experimenting with different formats or platforms. By maintaining a mindset of evolution, you can ensure that growth is sustainable, even in an unpredictable environment.

Building a Support Network

Isolation is a silent killer of growth. Trying to tackle every aspect of your business alone can lead to burnout and stagnation. Building a support network of peers, mentors, and collaborators can provide fresh perspectives, encouragement, and practical advice. Surrounding yourself with individuals who share your ambitions helps you stay motivated and accountable.

Communities also serve as a sounding board for ideas and a source of solutions. By engaging with others in your niche, you gain insights into their experiences and strategies for overcoming similar challenges. Collaboration, rather than competition, can open doors to opportunities you hadn't considered.

Sustaining Growth Through Innovation

Growth is not a one-time achievement; it is a continuous process fueled by innovation. Stagnation often sets in when you rely too heavily on what has worked in the past. While consistency is crucial for building trust with your audience, it must be balanced with fresh ideas that spark renewed interest.

Innovation doesn't always mean reinventing the wheel. Sometimes, it's as simple as repackaging existing content, introducing a new series, or finding unique ways to interact with your audience. Listening to feedback can guide your creative decisions, ensuring they align with the evolving desires of your community.

Nurturing Long-Term Vision

Growth, at its core, is about sustainability. Quick wins are enticing, but they rarely translate into lasting success. By focusing on long-term goals and staying true to your mission, you build a foundation that withstands the test of time. Regularly revisiting your vision and aligning your actions with it keeps you grounded and ensures that your growth trajectory remains steady.

Overcoming challenges and sustaining growth is less about avoiding failure and more about embracing it as a catalyst for progress. In the face of adversity, persistence and adaptability transform obstacles into opportunities, ensuring that your journey continues upward.

8.1 Navigating Algorithm Changes and Platform Updates

Understanding the Nature of Algorithms

Algorithms are the invisible hands that guide the content landscape, determining who sees what and when. For creators and entrepreneurs, they often feel like shifting sands—one moment, a post might reach thousands, and the next, it seems invisible. The key to navigating these changes lies in understanding that algorithms are not your enemy but tools designed to enhance user experiences. Their primary goal is to deliver content that resonates with audiences. By aligning your strategies with this principle, you can better anticipate shifts and adapt without losing momentum.

Each platform's algorithm operates differently, prioritizing engagement metrics such as likes, shares, comments, or watch time. While it's tempting to chase these metrics, focusing solely on them can lead to a diluted message. Instead, prioritize authenticity. Platforms consistently reward creators who foster meaningful connections with their audiences, regardless of algorithmic tweaks.

Adapting to Change Through Analytics

One of the most powerful tools in your arsenal is data. Analytics offer insights into what is working and what isn't, allowing you to pivot strategies when algorithms evolve. Regularly monitoring engagement metrics, audience demographics, and content performance ensures you're never caught off guard by sudden shifts.

For instance, if a platform begins favoring short-form videos, you might notice a decline in the reach of static posts. Instead of panicking, let the data guide you. Experiment with video content while keeping an eye on how your audience responds. Being proactive rather than reactive positions you as a creator who embraces change rather than resists it.

Diversifying Your Platform Presence

Relying on a single platform is a risk in a world where digital landscapes can change overnight. Algorithm updates on one platform might temporarily disrupt your reach, but having a presence on multiple platforms provides a safety net. Diversification doesn't mean spreading yourself too thin; it means strategically choosing platforms that align with your brand and audience.

Cross-promotion is a valuable strategy here. For example, use Instagram to drive traffic to your YouTube channel or blog, ensuring that even if one platform's algorithm changes, your overall visibility remains intact. By diversifying your digital footprint, you build resilience against unforeseen updates.

Fostering Direct Connections with Your Audience

While algorithms control the flow of content, they don't govern your relationship with your audience. Building direct lines of communication, such as email newsletters or private communities, ensures that you maintain control over how you reach your followers. Email lists, in particular, are a timeless tool for bypassing algorithmic barriers, offering a direct path to your audience's inbox.

Engaging meaningfully with your community fosters loyalty that transcends platform limitations. When your audience feels valued, they are more likely to seek out your content, even when algorithms make it less visible.

Embracing the Constant Evolution

Algorithm changes and platform updates are inevitable, but they are not insurmountable. Treat them as opportunities to refine your approach and deepen your connection with your audience. By remaining informed, flexible, and focused on delivering value, you transform algorithmic challenges into stepping stones for growth. The creators who thrive in this landscape are those who embrace change as an integral part of the journey, not a hindrance.

8.2 Dealing with Burnout and Maintaining Creativity

Recognizing the Signs of Burnout

In the race to grow a digital presence and sustain success, burnout often looms as a silent threat. It doesn't announce itself with fanfare; instead, it creeps in gradually, cloaked in feelings of exhaustion, diminished enthusiasm, and a sense of creative stagnation. Recognizing these signs early is vital. Perhaps you notice that the work you once loved feels more like a burden, or that the ideas which used to flow effortlessly now feel elusive. These are not just passing moments of fatigue—they are your mind and body signaling the need for recalibration.

Acknowledging burnout is not a weakness; it's an essential first step toward recovery. Ignoring it in the name of productivity often leads to diminished quality in your output and, more importantly, jeopardizes your well-being.

The Power of Pausing

When burnout strikes, the most counterintuitive but effective strategy can be to stop. Pausing doesn't mean failure; it means prioritizing your long-term potential over short-term gains. Take a step back to evaluate your workload, commitments, and creative process. Is there unnecessary pressure you've placed on yourself? Are there tasks that could be delegated or postponed?

During this pause, lean into restorative activities. Nature walks, meditation, reading, or simply spending time away from screens can work wonders in rejuvenating your mental clarity. Giving your mind the space to wander often leads to unexpected sparks of creativity. The pause isn't just about rest; it's about creating fertile ground for new ideas to take root.

Reconnecting with Your Why

One of the most effective antidotes to burnout is reconnecting with the purpose behind your work. Why did you start this journey in the first place? What impact did you hope to make? Reflecting on these questions can reignite your passion. Sometimes, the demands of algorithms, deadlines, and audience expectations can cloud your original vision.

Revisit old projects or posts that bring you joy. Reading heartfelt comments or remembering the positive changes you've inspired can rekindle your sense of purpose. By anchoring yourself to your "why," you create a wellspring of motivation that can withstand the pressures of growth and innovation.

Cultivating Sustainable Creativity

Creativity isn't a well that runs dry; it's a muscle that strengthens with care and use. To maintain creativity, establish habits that nurture your imaginative instincts. Set aside time for play—exploring new hobbies, learning unrelated skills, or experimenting with ideas without the pressure of perfection. Creativity thrives in spaces where failure isn't feared but embraced as part of the process.

Diversify your sources of inspiration. Seek out art, books, and conversations outside your usual sphere. Fresh perspectives can breathe life into your work and offer new angles to approach familiar subjects. Surround yourself with individuals who energize and challenge you, creating an environment where ideas flourish.

Building Resilience for the Long Term

Burnout doesn't have to be an inevitable part of success. By prioritizing self-care, setting boundaries, and fostering sustainable creative practices, you build resilience against its grasp. Remember that the best work often comes not from relentless hustle but from a balanced, inspired mind. Creativity, after all, is not a sprint—it's a marathon. Allow yourself the grace to rest, recover, and reimagine as you continue your journey toward sustained growth and fulfillment.

8.3 Tracking Metrics to Ensure Long-Term Success

Understanding the Power of Metrics

In the ever-evolving landscape of digital entrepreneurship, intuition alone isn't enough to navigate the path to long-term success. Metrics provide the critical insight needed to evaluate your strategies, identify what works, and pivot when necessary. Far from being just numbers on a dashboard, metrics are the heartbeat of your business, offering tangible evidence of growth, audience engagement, and profitability. By tracking the right data, you unlock the ability to make informed decisions and maintain a competitive edge.

The key is to focus on actionable metrics—those that align directly with your goals. Vanity metrics, such as follower counts or likes, can offer a quick dopamine hit, but they rarely reflect meaningful progress. Instead, prioritize metrics that tell a deeper story, such as conversion rates, retention rates, and customer lifetime value. These numbers are the true indicators of your impact and sustainability.

Choosing the Metrics That Matter

Every business has unique goals, and the metrics you prioritize should align with yours. If you aim to grow an engaged community, focus on metrics like comments, shares, and time spent engaging with your content. If revenue is your primary goal, metrics such as average order value, click-through rates, and revenue per customer take precedence.

Set benchmarks for these metrics, and compare your performance over time. For instance, a steady increase in email open rates signals that your content resonates with your audience, while a decline may indicate the need for more compelling subject lines or segmentation. These benchmarks serve as a roadmap, showing you where you are and where you need to go.

Adopting a Holistic Approach

While individual metrics provide valuable insights, true success lies in understanding how they interact. For instance, a spike in website traffic may seem positive at first glance, but if your bounce rate simultaneously increases, it's a sign that your content isn't aligning with visitor expectations. Similarly, if your conversion rates are high but your retention rates are low, it indicates that while you're good at attracting customers, you may need to improve your efforts to keep them engaged.

Holistic analysis requires looking at the bigger picture and connecting the dots between various data points. This approach not only helps you spot weaknesses but also reveals opportunities to optimize your strategy and enhance overall performance.

Leveraging Tools for Data Insights

Gone are the days when tracking metrics required manual effort. Today, an array of tools allows you to monitor performance with precision and ease. Platforms like Google Analytics, Instagram Insights, and email marketing dashboards offer comprehensive data tailored to your specific needs. These tools can automate reporting, provide trend analyses, and even offer predictive insights to guide your future strategies.

The true power of these tools lies in their ability to help you anticipate changes and adapt proactively. By regularly reviewing your metrics and integrating them into your decision-making process, you ensure that your business remains agile and prepared for both challenges and opportunities.

Committing to Continuous Improvement

Tracking metrics isn't a one-time task; it's an ongoing commitment to growth. Success is not a destination but a process of continuous refinement. As your business evolves, so will your goals and the metrics that matter most. Stay curious, stay flexible, and let your data guide you toward sustained success. By embracing a metrics-driven mindset, you position yourself not just to succeed today, but to thrive for years to come.

8.4 Building a Business That Outlasts Social Media

The Fragility of Platforms

Social media has become a cornerstone of modern business strategies, offering unprecedented opportunities to reach global audiences. Yet, these platforms are not immune to change. Algorithms shift, features disappear, and entire networks can fade into irrelevance. For businesses that rely solely on social media, such shifts can feel catastrophic, leading to a sudden loss of reach or revenue. To ensure longevity, it's essential to view social media not as the foundation of your business but as one of many tools in your arsenal.

Building a business that outlasts social media starts with creating a strong core. This core includes your unique value proposition, loyal audience, and diversified channels. By ensuring your business has a solid foundation beyond any single platform, you can navigate changes with resilience and thrive no matter how the digital landscape evolves.

Owning Your Audience

The greatest vulnerability of relying on social media is that you don't own your audience; the platform does. Followers, likes, and views are controlled by algorithms that can be altered overnight. To safeguard your connection with your audience, prioritize building an owned audience. Email lists, for example, are invaluable assets that allow direct communication with your community, free from third-party control.

Start by creating compelling lead magnets to encourage followers to join your email list. Whether it's a free guide, exclusive content, or early access to products, these incentives help you transition your audience from social media to a channel you own. Once you've built your list, nurture it with consistent, engaging content that reinforces your brand's value.

Diversifying Revenue Streams

A business tied too closely to a single platform is financially vulnerable. Diversification is a key strategy for long-term stability. Consider expanding your offerings beyond the confines of social media. This might mean launching an e-commerce site, creating a subscription service, or developing digital products like courses or eBooks.

Each new revenue stream strengthens your business by reducing reliance on any one source. If an algorithm change diminishes your reach, diversified income ensures you still have multiple avenues to sustain your business. Moreover, offering varied products or services allows you to meet the evolving needs of your audience, fostering loyalty and increasing lifetime value.

Establishing Your Brand's Legacy

A business built to last extends beyond trends. It focuses on creating a brand identity that resonates deeply with its audience. This involves defining a mission, voice, and visual aesthetic that remains consistent across all platforms and channels. Your brand should evoke trust and recognition, allowing you to build a reputation that withstands fluctuations in the digital world.

Storytelling plays a crucial role in this process. Share your journey, values, and vision through every piece of content you create. These authentic narratives humanize your brand and forge emotional connections, making your audience more likely to follow you wherever you go.

Embracing Innovation Without Dependence

Sustainability doesn't mean resisting change. It means being adaptable while staying rooted in your core values. As new platforms emerge, explore them strategically, ensuring they complement your existing efforts rather than becoming the sole focus. Innovation keeps your business relevant, but it should never come at the cost of stability.

Conclusion:

As we wrap up this guide, it's clear that building passive wealth through Instagram is not just about creating viral content or relying on fleeting trends. It's about crafting a long-term strategy that leverages the power of evergreen content, digital courses, and automated affiliate marketing. These pillars not only allow you to earn income on your terms but also create a business that sustains and grows over time.

Throughout this journey, we've explored how to tap into Instagram's massive potential while also creating systems that run in the background, generating income without requiring constant attention. The beauty of passive income is that it frees you from the daily grind, allowing you to focus on what truly matters: connecting with your audience, refining your craft, and scaling your business.

Creating evergreen content is your foundation. By developing valuable, timeless posts and resources that can be repurposed and shared continuously, you ensure your efforts don't go to waste. These pieces of content work for you long after they're published, driving traffic and engagement on autopilot. Coupled with digital courses, you not only create something that people can benefit from on their own time, but you also position yourself as an authority in your niche, increasing trust and credibility.

Affiliate marketing adds another layer of passive income, turning your recommendations into revenue streams. When integrated with your content and audience engagement, it becomes a seamless way to generate income without feeling "salesy." With the right automation tools and a clear strategy, your affiliate marketing efforts can continue to thrive even while you sleep.

But perhaps the most important takeaway from this guide is that success on Instagram—or any platform—is about consistency and authenticity. While algorithms may change and trends may come and go, a genuine connection with your audience, paired with valuable content and products, will always stand the test of time. Your success isn't dependent on one viral post or the whims of a social media algorithm. It's about building a brand that resonates deeply with your audience, one that stands firm in the face of change.

By diversifying your income streams, whether through courses, affiliate marketing, or other avenues, you're creating multiple paths to financial freedom. This not only protects you from sudden shifts in the digital landscape but also ensures that you continue to grow and evolve alongside your audience.

As you implement the strategies laid out in this book, remember that passive wealth is a marathon, not a sprint. It requires dedication, learning, and experimentation. But with patience and persistence, you will create a business that not only generates income but also offers you the freedom and lifestyle you've always dreamed of.

Thank you for embarking on this journey to build your Instagram-powered business. Now, it's time to take action and turn these insights into reality. Your future of passive wealth awaits.

www.ingramcontent.com/pod-product-compliance
Lightning Source LLC
La Vergne TN
LVHW062035060326
832903LV00062B/1670